Parenting Errors

"Finally, a Sensible Parenting Book!

Here is a book that is as well written as it is useful. Reading this book was remarkably illuminating and made me assess my own parenting as well as my relationship with my children.

It is written in a positive, reasonable style without judgement and with compassion for all involved in the family. I highly recommend the book."

-Brad Wilhelm

Parenting Errors: How to Solve Them is a perceptive and helpful guide to assist parents and caregivers by child psychologist Dr. Kerby T. Alvy, offering solutions for harried parents to calmly deal with the unpredictable behaviors of their children.

Parenting Errors details the mistakes parents often make when raising children. Alvy notes how parents should not be too lenient nor too authoritative with kids to make the most impact. Alvy advocates when parents make mistakes, they should take action to correct those actions in a productive way. Parenting Errors has useful steps that parents can take; such as to apologizing to children when they're wrong. He also advocates progressive parenting tips such as talking to a child to resolve a conflict together. Alvy's advice is common sense advice any wise parent should have no problem in assimilating. He adds statements of positive reinforcement which parents can recite to their children in frequent situations, such as during a child's temper tantrums. Parents can easily apply the clearly written advice, step-by-step to any tough parenting situation. Though Parenting Errors has script-like sentences parents can literally recite to kids, the book also addresses special parenting circumstances.

In a refreshing change from other parental advice books, Alvy addresses the different challenges faced by parents of color and how they were raised with more authoritarian parenting with corporal punishment. He wants minority parents to break the cycle of harsh parenting and embrace more non-violent resolutions to correct a child's misbehavior. He delves into the complicated history of African-American parenting since slavery with great sensitivity. Despite the past, Alvy advocates that African-American parents counteract the ugly legacy of corporal punishment in parenting dating back to slavery with positive affirmations to their children about Black pride.

Parenting Errors would be best for parents and caregivers who are dealing with troublesome toddlers or rebellious teenagers. Fans of modern parenting advice books such as The Conscious Parent by Shefali Tsabary would love Alvy's expertise as well. Even old-school parents who want to maintain control over their children will like the advice Alvy dispenses about how to admit their parenting mistakes to their kids while still exercising parental authority.

Parents who want to openly communicate with their kids will also appreciate the advice of Parenting Errors and can share the text with other parents in book clubs. This book would make a perfect gift for parents-to-be as well as current parents who may need a bit of extra guidance. Additionally, Alvy's book would be great for child psychologists who want to study the best current psychological methods to help parents and children. Parenting Errors: How To Fix Them is an insightful text that will help parents overcome mistakes to become the best parents they can be, resulting in having the best children they can have also.

Reviewed by: **Ella Vincent**
Pacific Book Review Star
Awarded to Books of Excellent Merit

Parenting Errors

How to Solve Them

By Dr Kerby T Alvy

Rev. date: 09/22/2017

To order additional copies of this book, contact:
Xlibris
1-888-795-4274
www.Xlibris.com
Orders@Xlibris.com
761310

CONTENTS

Other books
by Dr Kerby T Alvy

Guidebooks for Parents

The Positive Parent: Raising Healthy, Happy and Successful Children, Birth-Adolescence

The New Power of Positive Parenting: 16 Guidelines for Raising Healthy and Confident Children

The Power of Positive Parenting: 11 Guidelines for Raising Healthy and Confident Children

Parent Education Programs

The New Confident Parenting Program

(With Dr Camilla Clarke)

Parent Handbook

The Effective Black Parenting Program

(With Marilyn Marigna)

Parent Handbook

Instructor Manual

The Soulful Parent: Raising Happy, Healthy and Successful African American Children

(with Harris, Bell and Liggins)

Black Parenting: Strategies for Training

The Los Niños Bien Educados Program

(With Dr Lupita Montoya Tannatt)

Parent Handbook

Instructor Manual

Related Books

Putting Effective Parenting First

(In Press)

The CICC Discovery Tool

(With the CICC Staff)

Bringing Parenting Education into the Early Childhood Care and Education System

(With the CICC Staff)

Part I

This book is for any person who is currently in a parental relationship with a child or adolescent. It is also for those of us, like me, whose children are adults.

This is because everyone who has been a parent— biological, foster, adoptive, step or grandparent–has made some parenting error at one or numerous times during our parental regime.

The book is designed to help us solve such errors, and it is never too late to do so.

The poet Alexander Pope said, "To err is human." We parents are very, very human in this sense.

Indeed, erring in our relationships with children is a large part of our experience. Most of us were never taught how to be as errorless as possible in raising children.

In addition, raising children is arguably the most difficult job we will ever have, since being a parent involves many overlapping and interrelated responsibilities. We will closely examine these in the section "Parenting" so that we will not be so hard on ourselves for the errors we make or have made.

We will also be learning some of the better ways of relating to and raising children. The most creative and modern parenting programs will become available to us. Part II of the book is devoted to this type of practical education.

For now, let's explore the various types of errors that we parents are prone to make.

Types of Parental Errors

A parental error is something we have done or not done that impedes the healthy growth and development of our children.

The error can consist of a painful and inconsiderate comment about the child's appearance or abilities that eats away at a child's self-esteem as he or she is receiving it.

It can be an entire approach to child-rearing that goes on for years, which predisposes a child to a lifetime of difficulty and problems. These are errors of commission.

By contrast, errors of omission can consist of not acknowledging when our children are behaving in cooperative and respectful ways because that is the way they should behave or for some other reason for not praising or appreciating them and their behavior.

A multiyear approach, where very few limits are ever set on a child's day-to-day actions, can predispose a child to a lifetime of being selfish in relation to others.

These multiyear errors, in overall approach, have received much attention by child development and health professionals who have championed one approach or another. Behavioral scientists have conducted research on different approaches. Their work will be presented in the section on "Effective and Ineffective Parenting" to provide a fuller appreciation about what a parenting approach looks like. And with such information, we might even consider changing our current approach.

Parenting

Parenting refers to the process of raising children and covers a broad range of activities. It can be viewed as consisting of five interrelated responsibilities. These are

1. providing resources to maintain a family and home,

2. caring for the home,

3. protecting children,

4. physically and psychologically caring for children, and

5. advocating for children and connecting them to the community and the wider society.

Each of these responsibilities is complex, multifaceted, and time-consuming.

Let's look more closely at this nonpaying and lifelong job of parenting. This will provide us a perspective on our errors by exemplifying how inherently difficult raising children happens to be.

Resource Provision

These responsibilities include providing the whole spectrum of resources that are necessary to sustain and maintain a home and family: material resources (housing, clothing, appliances, furniture, toys, games, etc.); nutritional resources (food, drink); utility resources (gas, water, electricity); service resources (physical, dental, and mental health services, educational services); community resources (parks, stores, churches, etc.); cultural and recreational resources (films, music, art, etc.);

and communication resources (televisions, telephones, radios, newspapers, computers, cell phones, and other such devices).

Our education, occupation, and income greatly determine our ability to provide these resources, and this ability, in turn, has repercussions on our other functions. Where the ability to provide is great, there is greater opportunity for cultivating and enjoying the other functions. Where the ability is limited, there is less opportunity.

An important aspect of resource provision covers our consumption priorities. For example, do we choose to purchase or rent housing in a more prestigious and safe area at the expense of vacation and clothing luxuries or necessities, or do we choose to purchase an expensive car or customize a car at the expense of not paying for educational materials for children?

Another aspect of resource provision has to do with the work that most of us must do in order to afford family resources. The challenges of balancing work and family responsibilities are greater today than ever before, because the clear majority of parents are in the workforce, regardless of whether they work at home or outside of the home. This reality raises questions about who stays home when the kids are sick if both parents work outside of the home and whose career or job is more important regardless of the location of the work. These resource provision–related issues certainly have an impact on the errors by creating additional conflicts to manage.

Caring for the Home

These responsibilities involve such basics as home maintenance (cleaning, painting, gardening, plumbing, etc.), clothing maintenance (cleaning, washing, ironing, sewing, etc.), nutrition maintenance (shopping, cooking, dishwashing, etc.), and car maintenance (cleaning, repairing, etc.).

Caring for the home also involves the budgeting, management, and investment of monies. This includes the day-to-day management of funds as well as speculative investments and gambling.

Protecting Children

We parents are the persons who are responsible for protecting family possessions and resources. We are also responsible for protecting the family's physical, psychological, spiritual, ethnic, and cultural integrity from threats from the natural environment and from other persons, groups, and institutions.

The types of threats that we parents protect children and teens from are the following:

a. *Threats of bodily harm.* These include threats to a young child's existence, which occur because the child doesn't yet appreciate threats such as sticking hands into fires, running into streets, etc. It also includes threats from other persons, such as physical assaults and rapes, bullying, and threats from the development of substance use disorders.

Parents today must also be vigilant in protecting children from predators who may approach them on the Internet and through the various technological devices children may use. It is also very important that we protect our children from sexually transmitted diseases like HIV/AIDS.

b. *Threats of psychological harm.* These include the devaluation of a child's capabilities, characteristics, and appearance.

c. *Threats of peer harm.* Included here are associations with antisocial peers and peer groups (gangs) for which we parents must also be more watchful these days, as well as the previously indicated threats from bullying peers.

d. *Threats of social harm.* These include discrimination against children of different gender in social institutions, including the school.

e. *Threats of racial, ethnic, cultural, and spiritual harm.* These include the demeaning of the values and customs of our ethnic, cultural, sexual, or religious group.

f. *Threats of Internet and media harm.* One such threat has already been mentioned—children being approached by sexual predators over the Internet and through various devices. More subtle and insidious is the exposure to violence on television, films, and all forms of media. Such large-scale exposure is known to stimulate aggressive thoughts and actions in children, thereby culturally predisposing them to being aggressive and hurtful.

Harm to children in one area has repercussions in others. An infant who sustains head or brain injuries may become psychologically incapacitated and develop with a restricted range of intellectual abilities. A child who is harmed because his ethnic or religious group is demeaned may be unable to separate himself from the social, political, and economic causes of discrimination and develop a low sense of self-esteem.

Protective functions are carried out through our management of the child's physical, social, and psychological environments to diminish and buffer the encounters that they may have with potential harm.

Childproofing the kitchen, restricting access to unsafe play areas, controlling access to certain people, and influencing how children relate to potentially harmful people and institutions all fall within the realm of child protection. Also in this area is how we orient children to understand the commercial and often violent images that they are exposed to through television and other media forms.

Parents differ greatly in how they carry out these protective functions and the degree to which they are involved. Parents who cannot afford optimally safe living conditions and who themselves are victims of discrimination are by necessity very much involved. Those living in unsafe buildings, where lead-based paint chips are available for children to eat and where drug trafficking occur outside of apartment doors, have to be especially vigilant to protect children.

When a parent and child's racial, ethnic, sexual, or religious group is subject to prejudice, discrimination, and stereotyping, parents must work hard to buffer and protect children from these types of psychological and physical hazards.

Parental violations or negligence in carrying out protective responsibilities are considered as child abuses. Parents who beat and burn children are engaging in physical child abuse. Sexually abusing or exploiting children inflicts often irreparable psychological harm, as does the use of emotionally abusive comments and put-downs. These abuses are, of course, major parental errors.

Parents who are minimally concerned about their children's whereabouts or do not know how to supervise from afar are also putting them in harm's way.

Physical and Psychological Caring

This responsibility involves the use of physical and psychological methods to guide all aspects of a child's development: motor, sensory, perceptual, physical, thinking, language, social, emotional, moral, spiritual, sexual, cultural, and educational. This reality reflects that we are the first and major guidance counselors of our children's development.

Physical caring refers to such activities as feeding children, cleaning and dressing them, attending to their health needs, administering medical assistance, taking them to doctors and dentists, attending to their rest and sleep needs, etc.

Psychological caring includes nurturing children and providing them with warmth and acceptance; disciplining children and helping them learn the social appropriateness of behavior; grooming them to make them presentable; orienting them to appropriate gender functioning; teaching them about the world; assisting with their formal education; managing the crises that occur when children are hurt or disruptive; providing information and guidance about sexual functioning; and enculturation (i.e., inculcating moral, religious, ethical, and cultural values in children).

The distinction between physical and psychological caring being made here is not meant to indicate that they are separate and unrelated processes. For example, the manner in which infants are fed can greatly influence the child's sense of acceptance. If it is done warmly and with careful attention to the child, the child is likely to feel more accepted. If it is done matter-of-factly or mechanically, the child is more likely to feel rejected, though the child's physical needs are being met. Thus, the more focused activities that are part of physical caring are also activities through which parents can help meet a child's other needs.

We parents vary widely in how we physically and psychologically care for our children. This variability is a result of many interrelated factors. The child's temperament, health status, personality, sex, and stage of development influence our caring actions. So does our own temperament, personality, health status, sex, and stage of development. How we care is basically the result of the interaction between our children's unique characteristics and our own.

The presence or lack of presence of other family members carries some weight on how we care—so does our family's socioeconomic resources and the amount and kind of external stresses on our family. In addition, the total community and societal context we find ourselves in helps shape our caring.

Regarding enculturation, some of us are extremely involved and very conscious of how and what we teach our children about our people. Other parents are less aware and enculturate their children simply by the way they relate to them.

There is also variability in terms of those aspects of child development that parents feel a responsibility for guiding. For example, some parents do not see it as their responsibility to guide their children's religious or spiritual development.

There is also variability that results from ignorance. For example, a parent may feel responsible for helping a child with her/his sexual development but may not know how to introduce or carry out this kind of guidance.

Indeed, many parents undoubtedly turn away from attempting to guide various aspects of their children's development because they just don't know how to do it. And they don't know how to do it because no one's ever taught them.

Thus, errors of omission are certainly understandable. Indeed, all sort of parental errors of omission are the result of never being educated about what to do in raising children.

Advocating and Connecting

Children, and particularly young ones, need to be represented before various groups and institutions because they do not have the status or capability to represent themselves. By advocating and connecting, we parents serve as linkage persons between our children and other individuals, groups, and institutions.

Parents are the child's linkage persons to the family of origin and the extended family, to the world of childcare, to schools and other educational institutions, to health-care professionals, to the world of work, to law enforcement and welfare systems, to transportation and communication systems, to tradespersons, etc.

We may physically link them to these persons, groups, or systems, as when we personally transport them or provide them with television sets, telephones, computers, and various other communication devices.

Advocating and connecting also include making sure that our children receive adequate care and attention from health professionals, childcare personnel, educators, and other persons who have responsibilities for children.

As with the other four major responsibilities, we parents differ greatly in how we carry out these advocacy and interfacing functions and which we consider to be appropriate. Here, again, a reluctance to get involved may have to do with not being educated in how to be involved.

Bringing It All Together

Overriding these five parenting functions is the ability to organize and manage all five of them at the same time. And as would be expected, parents differ greatly in how they accomplish this overarching and potentially overwhelming feature of parenting.

In carrying out these five interrelated sets of responsibilities, families are organized in a variety of ways. In many families, the functions are shared by two parents, with one parent responsible for one set of functions and the other for a different set. In other cases, each parent shares in carrying out each function or different aspects of each function.

There are families where the parents purchase the assistance of others to carry out these functions. There are families where persons other than the parents fulfill some of these functions, such as grandparents, older children, relatives, friends, or even the state. And there are single-parent families where one person fulfills all five.

There are also more and more families reconstituted because of divorce or separation, where more than one set of parents are involved. Here, the sharing and organization are extremely complex and demanding. Here, again, the making of errors is not hard to imagine.

I trust—if you have taken the time to read this far—it is crystal clear that being a parent is an invitation to a life of making errors. It is also an invitation to a life of joy, as raising children can also be the greatest and most joyous of undertakings.

Of course, raising children is not the only activities that we parents are involved in.

To carry out our resource-provision function, most of us now must work. Our vocation or career brings us into contact with people and institutions that engage us psychologically in terms of career aspirations, disappointments, and achievements. These personal aspects of work can also influence parenting in many ways and especially what career expectations we have for our children.

In addition to work relationships, we often have friendships and civic and religious associations that require energy and cultivation. We have relationships with each other or, if a single parent, with a lover or significant other. And more and more parents have emotionally draining relationships with their elderly parents. These intimate relationships can greatly affect how we carry out our parenting responsibilities.

Finally, we parents have relationships with ourselves. We may be embedded in a network of family members, friends, and religious and work associates, but we are unique individuals. Cultivating our own individuality within this rich relationship mix can be just as challenging as carrying out our array of responsibilities.

Clearly, the job of parenting itself is an enormously difficult one, and it is a job that is embedded in a variety of other relationships and societal demands. These realities (it is worth repeating) help us to more fully appreciate why we parents are so prone to making errors.

Solving Parental Errors: The AAR Approach

The approach to solving errors that is recommended here is the *AAR approach*.

The first *A* means we must *admit* to ourselves and our children that we have made an error. This requires a great deal of courage. But it is the best way to start to turn things around with children.

The second *A* means we must *apologize* to our children for our mistake.

Start by saying something like "I need to talk with you about some difficulties I have been having with how I treat you. Specifically, I want to apologize to you for calling you lazy, not listening to your side, making faces when you try to explain yourself, not picking you up from school on time, not being very positive in how I speak to you, etc."

Pause to see and hear your child's reactions. If the child questions you as to why you have made such a mistake, do your best about explaining yourself. Do not blame the child.

As to the *R*, it is now time to try to restore or reimburse the child for the damage you have done. It is time to make *restitution* (a making good of or giving an equivalent for some injury).

This should include your plan for avoiding similar errors in the future.

Of course, you should say you will try not to make the same or similar error in the future. But that is not enough.

Show that you have given this serious consideration and that you want to make up for your error in a more heartfelt and concrete way.

If you have said something unkind to your child, say that you will do some reading about how to better express yourself when you are feeling like being critical or unkind.

Or you will consult a counselor or psychotherapist to help you learn why you have been feeling critical and expressing unkind words.

Say you will be getting a book on good parenting, will be watching a show, or will be taking a parenting class.

Show the child something concrete that reflects the specifics of your plan, like an ad for the book or the book itself or an ad for a class you will take online or at a community college.

The book that is most obviously relevant is the one you are reading now.

You could mention that the author of this book is a nationally recognized expert on parenting, that he has been successfully running a parent education organization for over forty years, and that his children are now adults who are leading good lives and who were very good students, eventually earning a doctorate and a master's degree. Also, the author has made his share of errors and has found it helpful to admit, apologize, and restore.

Another good reason for choosing this book, especially if one of your errors has been your difficulty in expressing positive feelings to your children, is that it teaches some very fine methods for being positive, such as the effective praise, encouragement, and positive I-message methods.

This book also provides education about a wide range of parenting programs that can be used to learn multiyear positive-parenting approaches. These programs are not only described here but you are also oriented how best to take advantage of what they teach and how to locate them in your community. In addition, you will also learn how to locate counselors and psychotherapists.

This extensive array of opportunities to improve your life can be found in subsequent sections and especially in Part II of the book on "Effective Parenting Resources."

Here is a template you can use when you decide to use the AAR approach with your children:

Admit—indicate the parenting error or errors you are making or have made:_____

_____

_____

_____

_____

_____

Apologize—indicate the wording you will use as you apologize to your child for your errors:_____

_____

_____

_____

_____

Restore or make restitution—indicate the specifics of your plan for avoiding similar future mistakes:_____

_____

_____

_____

_____

_____

Please email me at _kalvy@ciccparenting.org_ to discuss your experiences in using this method. I look forward to hearing about how it goes!

Effective and Ineffective Parenting

Based on what we learned about the various responsibilities of being a parent, it is quite possible for any parent to be effective in one area of responsibility and less effective in another area. For example, someone could be a very effective resource provider but much less effective in physical and psychological caring.

It is also possible for a parent to be very effective in one part of an area and less effective in another. Here, an example would be a parent who is excellent about guiding his/her children's educational development. He/she is careful about which childcare and preschool people he/she uses, and he/she spends time relating to the staff to ensure that his/her child is well treated and understood. This same parent is likely to be just as involved in every educational setting that the child enters.

But that same parent could be much less effective at guiding the child's religious development. He/she may have been brought up himself/herself in a home where religion did not play much of a role or where the religion was oppressive to him/her. For whatever reasons, that parent is likely to be a poor guider of the child's growth and understanding of religious matters.

Now let's explore what professionals from the fields of mental health and child development have to say about overall parental effectiveness and ineffectiveness.

Because the focus of our book is on ineffective parenting, which we have referred to as *multiyear parenting errors*, we will begin there. Recall—such errors of parenting style place children at high risk for negative life outcomes.

After reviewing these errors, we will look at the parenting style that has been repeatedly associated with many positive life outcomes for children—the *authoritative parenting style*. We will refer to that style as a *multiyear positive parenting style*.

That style was first noted in the 1960s research studies of child developmental expert, Diana Baumrind. That is, of course, the style that is strongly recommended for anyone who wants to have the odds on their side about doing the best job possible in parenting.

This section will close with a description and examples of two of the very powerful skills for providing children with positive consequences. These skills can be used in restoring a relationship where there were commission errors of having made mean comments to children. They also are very useful in restoring a relationship for such omission errors as having neglected to provide positive reactions for their good behaviors. The skills are *effective praising* and *encouragement*.

Multiyear Parenting Errors

The first six such errors are those that emerge out of the many years of mental health work of social worker and psychotherapist John Lehman. They are part of his parenting program called the *Total Transformation Program*. The descriptions provided here were written by one of his coworkers—Megan Devine, LCPC. First, the name of the particularly error-filled style is given and then described, and then there are suggested ways of avoiding its damaging impact.

1A. *The overnegotiator.* This is an ineffective parenting style that many of us can identify with. If you allow your child to discuss consequences, boundaries, and rules—often succeeding in getting you to skew the rules in their favor—you might be an over negotiator. These parents may agree to a lighter consequence after an inappropriate behavior just because the child talks them into it. As James Lehman says, "Your child becomes an expert at pushing boundaries because he knows they can be changed." If you fall into this ineffective parenting style, you're probably accustomed to arguments and debates over the fairness of rules and whether your expectations are valid.

1B. *Solution.* The overnegotiating parents need to be firm about their rules, expectations, and consequences. Don't allow your children to change the rules or let them negotiate for a different consequence after the fact. By staying firm and clear, you help your children become accountable for their actions.

2A. *The screamer.* The parents who end up screaming and yelling at their children are often acting out from deep frustration and exhaustion. While understandable (most parents have been there), the fact is that losing your temper is unlikely to result in positive behavior changes in your children. If you get drawn into screaming matches, name-calling, or using threats, the message that you are sending to your children is that you are not in control. What this means is that your authority is jeopardized. It's as if, for that moment, you have come down to your children's behavioral level. The moms or dads stuck in this ineffective parenting style can even find themselves drawn into defending their own behavior; their children can easily deflect their own behavior issues by pointing out how badly their parents are behaving.

2B. *Solution.* The screamer parents need to learn more effective ways to handle their own frustration and annoyance. We get worn down (or worked up) and snap sometimes. It's part of the territory of parenting. But unless you get a handle on your own temper, your children are unlikely to see you as the calm, clear authority they need in order to get their behavior in check.

3A. *The martyr.* These parents never want to see their child fail or feel distress. If you want to protect your child from difficult emotions, you might work tirelessly to be sure that he or she doesn't feel left out or frustrated. You might find yourself working harder on homework or projects than your child does. You want the road ahead to be as smooth as possible for your child. How can this be bad?

The thing is, when you rush into doing things for your children, what you are doing is sending a message that you don't think that they are capable of handling the situation on their own. And that may be true! You might be worried that they can't do it. But the truth is—and this is important—kids learn problem-solving skills as they fail. They learn to handle feelings of frustration only if they get to experience frustration. If you make the road too easy for your children, protecting them against every feeling of failure or frustration, you are keeping them from learning their own strength. And you're exhausting yourself in the process!

3B. *Solution.* The martyr needs to stop working so hard. Allow your child to feel unhappy and frustrated. You can help him find ways to manage those feelings, but don't shield him from them. Ask yourself, "Am I doing something that my child can really do for himself?"

4A. *The perfectionist.* The perfectionist parents can be seen as the flip side of the martyr. Instead of seeing everything their child does as great, these parents see everything their child does as not good enough. Parents stuck in this ineffective parenting style know their kids have great talents; they just need to work harder at them. So why would that be ineffective? Because the perfectionist parents teach the children that failure is expected from them. If children can never measure up to the high standards their parents have for them, why should they even try? And if the children are successful, the perfectionist parents will often raise the bar, insisting that their children can do even better next time.

Perfectionist parents often feel they know their children so well, and that they know what they're thinking. They often assume the worst, detecting their children assumed bad attitude even before they open their mouth. Why is this ineffective? Unfortunately, what you're teaching your children is to never show their emotions, to keep any accomplishments to themselves, and to avoid interacting with you. Why? Because they know they will never be good enough. You're not teaching your children to reach their potential; you're teaching them to cringe at every correction.

4B. *Solution.* The perfectionist parents need to allow some distance between themselves and their child—at least between their expectations and their child's actual interests. Negative pressure, scolding, and hypercriticism won't make kids improve. Encouraging your child to reach her goals and explore her natural talents is a much better atmosphere for growth.

5A. *Bottomless pockets.* The parents with bottomless pockets are those who hope to make a connection with their children by giving them whatever they want. We see this often in families where the children may spend time with two different sets of parents/stepparents, but it can certainly happen within one household too. The bottomless-pocket parents, or "over givers," indulge children materially, often to stop the children's behavior problems or to prevent future ones. As James Lehman writes in the *Total Transformation*, "It's often easier for the parent to spend money – even money they don't have – than it is to suffer the reactions when their child hears 'no.'"

What this does is create a false sense of entitlement in your children. They learn to manipulate you into giving them what they want. Because it feels easy to get material goods, the children do not learn the reality of having to work for rewards or compensation. This can set them up not only for future problems in the adult work world but also in setting and achieving their own personal goals.

5B. *Solution.* The parents with bottomless pockets need to learn to say no—and to tolerate their children's reactions when they don't get what they want. If you want to use material things as rewards for your child, be sure they relate to tangible expectations, effort, and accomplishments, not simply just because they asked.

6A. *The ticket puncher.* The parents stuck in this ineffective role act like their child's best friends. They go overboard trying to understand their child's needs and motivation, often identifying quite deeply with their child. For example, if you didn't enjoy school as a child, you may trivialize or minimize your child's poor school behavior. After all, you *understand* what he's going through. The ticket-puncher parents side with the child in most circumstances, joining him/her in badmouthing authority figures or ignoring rules he/she finds unimportant.

The problem with this style of parenting is not that you *understand* your child; it's that you let your *understanding* keep you from following the rules. The child does not need to manage her behavior if she can convince you that her reasons are valid or that it is someone else's fault. The parents may then blame other people's negative influence on their child, rather than see their child as wholly responsible for his/her own actions.

6B. *Solution.* The ticket-punching parents need to make a clear distinction between understanding their children and holding them accountable for their actions. Just because you can *relate* to your children's frustration does not mean they don't have to follow the rules. You can be compassionate while also being clear about your expectations for their behavior.

The next two styles are from the Baumrind studies. They are styles that have been found to be much less effective than the *authoritative style* that we are using as the gold standard of parenting styles (i.e., the style that has been found to be the most effective in raising children). That style will be defined below and referred to as a *multiyear positive parenting style.*

The other two styles that Baumrind explored she referred to as the *permissive* and *authoritarian* styles. They have been associated with some positive outcomes in the lives of children. But most of the outcomes that have been found to be related to these styles have been negative. For example, *permissively* reared children are more likely to be rebellious and defiant when their desires are challenged, show low persistence on dealing with challenging tasks, and engage in more antisocial behaviors. Children raised through the *authoritarian style* tend to have anxious, withdrawn, and unhappy dispositions and have poor reactions to frustration. Here are descriptions of these two less positive approaches:

7. The *permissive* parents attempt to behave in a nonpunitive, acceptant, and affirmative manner toward the child's impulses, desires, and actions. These parents consult with the child about policy decisions and give explanations for family rules. These parents make few demands for household responsibility and orderly behavior. They present themselves to the child as a resource for him to use as he wishes—neither as an ideal for him to emulate nor as an active agent responsible for shaping or altering his ongoing or future behavior. These parents allow the child to regulate his own activities as much as possible, avoid the exercise of control, and do not encourage children to obey externally defined standards. *Permissive* parents attempt to use reason and manipulation but not overt power to accomplish their ends.

8. The *authoritarian* parents attempt to shape, control, and evaluate the behaviors and attitudes of their children in accordance with a set standard of conduct, usually an absolute standard—theologically motivated and formulated by a higher authority. These parents value obedience as a virtue and favors punitive, forceful measures to curb self-will at points where the child's actions or beliefs conflict with what they consider is a right conduct. The authoritarian parents believe in keeping the child in their place, in restricting his autonomy, and in assigning household responsibilities in order to inculcate respect for work. These parents regard the preservation of order and traditional structure as a highly valued end in itself. Authoritarian parents do not encourage verbal give-and-take, believing that the child should accept their word for what is right.

A Multiyear Positive Parenting Style

Here is the *authoritative style*:

First and possibly foremost, this style is reflected in and defined by *parents who convey a great deal of parental acceptance and warmth in how they talk to, touch, and relate to their children.* These are parents who regularly seek out and enjoy the company of their children and who are satisfied with their children and their characteristics and abilities. *They are sensitive to their children's needs and viewpoints, and they provide a great deal of positive reinforcement.*

In addition, parents who approach their children in this style *are fair and firm in their disciplinary actions.* They clearly explain what is expected of their children and set very clear limits on their children's behavior. *They are vigilant about enforcing family rules, thereby establishing their authority and providing standards by which their children can judge their competence and progress.* They use commands and sanctions when necessary and do not give in to children's coercive demands.

Parents who use and reflect this style also make age-appropriate demands on their children for mature behavior. For example, expecting a ten-year-old not to have temper tantrums where they fall on the floor and kick and scream is an age-appropriate demand or expectation. Expecting a two-year-old toddler to always express frustration without having a tantrum is not an age-geared demand, because a child that young has very few other means of expressing intense feelings.

These parents are also very responsive to the cues emanating from their children's behavior, beginning by being sensitive to the movements and cries of infants and continuing to be responsive and sensitive to the behavior of older children and teenagers.

This style is further characterized by parents who are very much involved in the lives of the children, demonstrating how important the children are to them. These parents make their children a priority in their lives.

Research study after research study has shown that this style of parenting is consistently associated with and contributes to children becoming

- independent,

- highly competent in social and academic pursuits,

- socially responsible,

- able to control aggression,

- self-confident,

- popular with peers and others, and

- high in self-esteem.

In addition, studies that have followed these authoritatively parented children into adulthood have shown that they are most likely to have successful careers and healthy marriages.

Thus, this style, which has the most support from scientific studies of parenting styles, is the one that is being so strongly recommended here. It is also the style that is taught in the modern parenting skill-building programs that will be described in Part II on "Effective Parenting Resources."

Providing Children with Positive Consequences

These are two of the best and most powerful ways of conveying warmth and acceptance of children. They are great ways to make amends for errors and for facilitating a good relationship. Use them and you will not be disappointed.

Effective Praise

The first is the *effective-praising method* or the art of effective praising. It is a systematic method for insuring that your praise not only conveys warmth and appreciation but also instructs your children about what you consider to be acceptable or appropriate behavior. When you teach your children what you consider to be acceptable behavior, you are also teaching them your family values.

Values need to be practiced for them to become real for children. If you value cooperation and you behave in cooperative ways by helping others or helping around the house, your children will see that your value of cooperation is for real.

When you use this method of praising your children, you are helping to teach your children family values. The specific behaviors that you praise are behaviors that reflect your values. *Praising children when they play or work together cooperatively or when they pick up after themselves or when they speak in a respectful tone of voice is demonstrating in your parenting that you value cooperation, responsibility, and respect for others.*

The use of the effective-praising method requires that you must catch your kids being good. Then you are ready to use the seven steps of effective praising:

1. Look at your child.

2. Move close to your child.

3. Smile!

4. Say lots of nice things to your child.

5. Praise behavior, not the child.

6. Be physically affectionate.

7. Move into action immediately.

The first three steps are concerned with the body language of delivering effective praising:

1. *Look at your child.* Before you can praise a child effectively, you must look at the child. This lets the child know that you are talking to him or her.

2. *Move close to your child.* This increases the power of praise because it is so much more personal and intimate.

3. *Smile!* Sometimes just a smile is rewarding enough by itself to make another person feel good. So you can imagine how powerful a smile can be when it's coupled with lots of praise.

Now what do we say?

4. *Say lots of nice things to your child*. The idea here is to make a big deal out of what your child is doing—to shower the child with attention and say a lot of nice things, such as the following:

- Thank you!

- That's nice!

- Good job!

- Good thinking!

- I really like it when you speak to me in that tone of voice!

- That really pleases me!

5. *Praise behavior, not the child*. This is a really important step: be sure to praise behavior and not the child.

In other words, praise your child for what he/she does, not what the child may be. There's a world of difference, for example, between saying "It was nice of you to help me do the dishes, Britt" and saying "You are such a good girl, Britt."

The first conveys the message that Britt earned praise for her cooperative behavior—washing the dishes. The second statement is merely an opinion or judgment about Britt as a person and does not give any information about what she did to merit that high opinion.

The last two steps are concerned with showing affection and with the best time to deliver effective praising.

6. *Be physically affectionate*. A hug, a kiss, or a hand on the shoulder will go a long way toward making your praise

something warm and special to your child. Don't be afraid to show your affection. Get physical with your children when you praise them.

7. *Move into action immediately.* It's important to praise right when you recognize desirable behavior. If you have "caught" your child helping to clean the table, praise the child right away. Don't save it for later in the day or even five minutes.

So now you have it—all seven steps and guidance on how to carry them out. Thousands of other parents who have learned this seven-step *effective praise method* have reported excellent results. Their kids really like being treated this way, and they appreciate being acknowledged for doing the right things. Some children even start praising their parents!

This is one of the methods that are taught in the *New Confident Parenting program* and in the versions of that skill-building program for African and Latino American parents, the *Effective Black Parenting* and *Los Niños Bien Educados* programs (these are some of the programs that will be described in Part II of our book). When used within the latter two programs or with any family or culture that has developed their own unique ways of expressing appreciation, those expressions can be used in terms of what to say when you praise.

For example, in many homes of African American children, appreciation is expressed through the use of such expressions as "On the one!" or "Hey, that's too tough!" or "Go, girl/go, boy!" or "Get on down!" or "Let's have five!" Using cultural or family-specific expressions adds new dimensions to your praise, reflecting that everyone in your group is appreciative of how the child is acting.

The Encouragement Method

This approach to conveying warmth is taught in such parenting skill-building programs like *Active Parenting* and *Systematic Training for Effective Parenting (STEP).* It not only conveys warmth and acceptance but it also helps children learn from their mistakes without dwelling on them. It helps them learn to believe in themselves and their abilities.

For example:

A child has missed five out of twenty-five words on a spelling test. Instead of dwelling on five errors, a parent who uses and believes in encouragement would point out the twenty words that were spelled correctly.

By focusing on the positive, the parent gives the child the feeling that she is okay. The child is well aware of the five errors; there is no need to point them out.

Accepting the child helps her feel worthwhile as a person.

Learning and using *encouragement* are particularly important if you have been in the habit of engaging in the parental error of discouraging children.

You discourage children when you have unreasonably high standards, such as when you expect them to do well in all endeavors or to have every hair on their head in place or to expect their rooms or personal spaces to be as neat as a pin.

You also discourage children when you promote competitions between brothers and sisters or have double standards where you expect cleanliness from some children in the family but not others.

Using encouragement means emphasizing the positive. It means using phrases that show acceptance of a child and phrases that recognize effort and improvement, such as the following:

"I like the way you handled that."

"I like the way you tackle a problem."

"I'm glad you enjoy learning."

"I'm glad you are pleased with it."

"It looks as if you enjoyed that."

The *encouragement method* also involves using communications and phrases that show confidence:

"Knowing you, I'm sure you'll do fine."

"You'll make it!

"I have confidence in your judgment."

"That's a rough one, but I'm sure you'll work it out."

"You'll figure it out."

Encouragement also entails focusing on the contributions that children make and showing appreciation through such statements as the following:

"Thanks, that helped a lot."

"It was thoughtful of you to . . ."

"Thanks, I really appreciate _____ because it makes my job easier."

"I need your help on . . ."

To a family group—"I really enjoyed today. Thanks."

"You have skill in _____. Would you do that for the family?"

A very important part of using the *encouragement method* is recognizing children's efforts and improvements through such communication as the following:

"It looks as if you really worked hard on that."

"It looks as if you spent a lot of time thinking it through."

"I see that you're moving along."

"Look at the progress you've made." (Be specific, tell how.)

"You're improving in . . ." (Be specific.)

"You may not feel that you've reached your goal, but look how far you've come!"

Note of Caution

These and the other encouraging communications you have been learning can be discouraging to children when they are used with an "I told you so" or an arrogant attitude. Avoid giving with one hand and taking away with the other. In other words, avoid qualifying or moralizing comments.

For example, avoid such communications as the following:

"It looks like you really worked hard on that—so why not do that all the time?" or "It's about time" or "See what you can do when you try?"

Remember, an important reason for using encouragement is to show faith in your children so that they can come to believe in themselves. Using this method is an excellent way of accepting them as they are, pointing out the positive aspects of their behavior, recognizing effort and improvement, and showing appreciation for their contributions.

In learning *effective praising* and the *encouragement method*, you are learning skills and ideas that you can also put to work in your relationships with other adults.

Most human beings appreciate being praised and encouraged and feel kindly toward those who recognize their positive actions and efforts. You can use these skills with your spouse, other family members, friends, coworkers, and employers. Thus, you can gain other relational benefits for having put in the time and effort to learn how to use these skills properly and frequently.

And think how you have come to be exposed to these relational benefits—by wanting to avoid parenting errors!

You will be exposed to even more great ways of improving your relationships as we turn to look at many of the other resources that are available to you to deal with all sorts of parenting errors.

Part II

Effective Parenting Resources

Most of what is needed to know about avoiding all types of parenting errors comes from our nation's parenting skill-building programs, which is where the *effective praising* and the *encouragement method* came from.

We will begin by gaining an overview of these skill-enhancing programs and learn where to find them and how best to relate to them. Several program descriptions contain detailed descriptions of parenting skills, which should make it easier for you to learn and use them.

Parenting and Family Skill-Building Programs

Let's start with a little history. The importance of educating parents to be as effective as possible in raising children has been recognized in the United States since at least 1815, when the first parent group meetings were reported. These and other early efforts allowed groups of parents to gain emotional and social support from each other and to learn about child development.

In the late 1960s, a new approach to educating and training parents emerged—the creation and use of carefully constructed parenting and family skill-building programs. The first program of this nature that became widely known and widely used was the *Parent Effectiveness Training (PET)* program created by psychologist Dr. Thomas Gordon. We will learn more about this program in this section.

Parenting skill-building programs are designed to improve parental effectiveness by providing a clear parenting philosophy and a series of positive parenting skills and strategies that can be used immediately to address a variety of child-rearing challenges and problems. What these excellent programs teach and promote is consistent with the *authoritative parenting style.* It is no wonder then that studies that evaluate the impact of these programs on children, parents, and families consistently find that these programs do the following:

- Increase parental confidence

- Reduce parental stress and anxiety

- Improve parenting skills

- Reduce or eliminate spanking and hitting

- Improve parent-child relations

- Reduce child's behavioral problems

- Improve child's cooperation

- Improve child's self-esteem

- Improve child's adjustment

- Improve child's academic performance

- Strengthen families

These programs bring people together in groups. Most are designed for groups of parents although some also include children. Those versions are best understood as family skill-building programs. That is so because the children are also trained and educated to use new skills and ideas about how best to relate to their parents and other people.

Types of Programs

In general, these programs fall into five major categories:

General parenting skill-building programs. These are programs that have been designed for any parent, regardless of the age of his or her children and regardless of cultural or religious background. Examples are the *PET* program, a version of *family effectiveness training,* and the *New Confident Parenting program.*

Age-related parenting skill-building programs. These are designed for parents of children of different ages. Included here are *Active Parenting,* with its versions for parents of young children called *1, 2, 3, 4 Parents!* and its program for parents of elementary school children *Active Parenting Now;* and its program for parents of teenagers *Active Parenting of Teens. Systematic Training for Effective Parenting (STEP)* also has age-related versions such as *Early Childhood STEP, STEP, and STEP Teen.* The *Incredible Years* is designed for parents of children in the four to eight age range.

Population-specific parenting skill-building programs. These include such culturally specific, general skill-building programs, as *CICC's Effective Black Parenting* for parents of African American children and *CICC's Los Niños Bien Educados* for parents of Latino American children. Also, included here are parenting programs or versions of programs that have been created for different religious denominations, such as the versions of *Active Parenting for Christian and Jewish* denominations and the version of *STEP for Christian* settings. In addition, there is the *Nurturing Program for Teenage Parents and Their Families.*

Topic-centered skill-building programs. These focus on major child-rearing issues and provide in-depth approaches and assistance. Good examples are the *Siblings Without Rivalry* program that provides numerous ways of understanding and productively dealing with this common and challenging phenomenon. The *Stop and Think* program helps teach children basic social skills to use in their relationships with others, including their relationships with teachers. Another example of a topic-specific program is the *Parents on Board* program that helps you to be a good coach for your children regarding their formal education.

Family skill-building programs. These are programs that include your children in the training. Groups of families participate at the same time, usually in sessions where they are all together and in sessions where there is training for just parents and for just children. A good example is the *Strengthening Families* program. Another example would be the previously mentioned *Nurturing* programs, because those population-specific programs are designed to be taught to both parents and children.

All these programs are usually taught by professional instructors who have received specialized training in how best to teach or facilitate them. These instructors include social workers, educators, psychologists, child and family counselors, nurses, parent-involvement coordinators, and prevention specialists. These are our neighbors who have committed themselves to a helping profession and have taken it upon themselves to receive additional education and training to be knowledgeable and skillful in helping us be more effective with our children.

These programs can be taken in person as classes or seminars. Some are also available to be taken on line.

Where the Programs Can Be Found

These knowledgeable neighbors mainly teach the programs through the agencies, schools, and organizations that employ them, such as child guidance centers, schools, Head Start agencies, mental health and drug abuse treatment agencies, hospitals, and child welfare agencies. Indeed, nearly every private organization that serves children and families in a community has determined that their missions can best be accomplished when parents are skillful and humane in raising children. So by hiring or training personnel who can deliver parenting and family skill-building programs, these helpful organizations have another means to carry out their mandated missions.

Trained instructors also find themselves offering these programs through the religious organizations of which they are a part of or with which they consult. Some also offer the programs through their private practices or through employee assistance and wellness programs or health-maintenance organizations.

Program Formats

Skill-building programs are taught through different formats. Sometimes they are taught as multisession parenting classes, all-day seminars, or one-session meetings.

Multiple-session parenting classes. These classes meet once or twice a week for anywhere from six to twenty weeks.

Here, all the program's parenting skills, strategies, and concepts are presented and discussed, and a variety of methods—such as role-playing, instructor demonstration, and lecturing—are used to educate about how best to use the skills and ideas with children. These classes are for small numbers of parents (ten to twenty-five) and are akin to a college practicum or a small group seminar. Parents receive homework assignments where they use the skills with their children, and then they report back to the group and receive further technical assistance and support from both the instructor and from the other parents.

One-day seminars. Here, only some of the program skills and concepts are taught. These seminars are for large numbers of parents (fifty to two hundred).

One-session meetings. These include lunch-and-learn meetings in work settings where one or two program skills are taught or where a specific topic from the program is covered.

The longer, more intense teaching formats—the multiple-session classes—are generally the most effective because you have more time to learn and practice the skills and to integrate the parenting ideas and values into your overall approach to parenting.

These more intense and intimate training formats also allow for a good deal of mutual support and understanding among parents. They often lead parents to exchange phone numbers and continue to meet and help each other.

This bonding and support is even more likely to happen when the program is for groups of parents who have much in common, such as parents of children with the same age range, parents from the same cultural or religious group, or parents who all have children with special needs.

The briefer formats—the one-day seminars and one-session meetings—are helpful because they give you at least one or two good ideas and some skill training that can be used immediately with your children. They can also motivate you to want to take and learn the entire program once you have realized how much you and your family can gain from this type of education.

Making the Most of Programs

The first thing you need to do is find a program that relates to your current parenting needs. This requires that you have some knowledge of what the programs teach. Further in this part, you will be able to gain a good deal of program knowledge.

As part of the programs you select, you will receive a handbook that covers what is taught, and it will have homework assignments in it. Read each section as it is assigned. Having the handbook available after you have completed the program allows you to refresh your knowledge when you keep it around the house for frequent reference.

Another thing you can do to increase the power of the program is to have a good attitude about participating. You are the most knowledgeable person about your children and your home situation, so you are the authority on parenting your children. But don't let that reality stand in the way of learning additional ideas about parenting and new skills or finding out that you have not been doing as good a job as possible. Have an open mind. Try out the ideas and use the skills, do the homework assignments, and don't fight this learning opportunity.

It is also wise to attend every class session of the multisession programs, as these programs are carefully organized so that a parenting skill or concept that you learn in one session provides a foundation and justification for what you will be learning in subsequent sessions.

If you miss a session, try to take it over if the program is being taught nearby, talk to the instructor, or talk to your fellow parents to bring yourself up to speed.

One of the things that these programs teach is to be very positive with your children and to show appreciation for their efforts and appropriate behaviors. Your instructor and the agency or organization that hosts or sponsors your class, seminar, or workshop also deserves similar treatment. Let them know how grateful you are for this opportunity. Like your children, they are then more likely to continue to make your life easier when you treat them well.

Also, share what you are learning with other family members, friends, and coworkers. Word of mouth from someone who has experienced the benefits of becoming an educated parent is the most powerful advertising and endorsement possible.

Other Group Parenting Education Experiences

In addition to classes and seminars in these carefully organized parenting skill-building programs, there are a variety of other parenting education experiences that often are provided by community organizations. For example, religious and other community organizations frequently sponsor *mommy-and-me* and *daddy-and-me* classes, where parents bring their young children to learn how best to relate to and enjoy each other. Many schools offer other types of parenting classes through their adult or parent education departments.

Individualized Parenting Education and Support

Some communities now are in the habit of providing parenting education on a one-to-one basis.

Home visiting. Home visiting involves having a trained service provider visit parents of newborns and young children in their homes to educate and support them in being effective and humane in raising their babies and youngsters. The home visitor supplies emotional support and authoritative child development information, teaches parenting skills, and facilitates a family's connection to other community services that they may need. Home visiting is an extraordinarily friendly and personal service.

Several home-visiting efforts emerged out of the health fields and were initially developed for providing families who are at high risk for abusing their babies with special support and education. Possibly the most widely used and known of these types of home visiting is the *Nurse Home Visiting* program created by Dr. David Olds, a professor of pediatrics, psychiatry, and preventive medicine at the University of Colorado.

Since 1977, Dr. Olds has been developing and testing his approach to home visiting—called the Olds Model—and it has proven to be extremely successful in educating high-risk, low-income mothers to be very effective with their children. Dr. Olds' exemplary work has blossomed into the *Nurse-Family Partnership*, a nonprofit organization serving more than thirty thousand mothers in thirty states across the nation. From the organization's website www. nursefamilypartnership.org, you will be able to learn more about the overall program and find the groups closest to your home that are providing home-visiting services. The program's emphasis is on working with first-time parents.

Another national home-visiting effort that originated to prevent child maltreatment is *Healthy Families America*. It is designed to help expectant and new parents give their children a healthy start. This home-visiting effort was launched in 1992 by Prevent Child Abuse America (formerly known as the National Committee to Prevent Child Abuse).

Families participate voluntarily in the program, and Healthy Families America programs now exist in over five hundred communities in the United States and Canada. You can learn more about this highly effective effort and locate the closest Healthy Families America organization by visiting the program's website, www.healthyfamiliesamerica.org.

Another nationally prominent home-visiting effort emerged out of the education field and is directed more at providing parents with information, skills, and supports to help guide their young children's educational growth. The best known of this variety of home visiting is *Parents as Teachers*. It originated in Missouri and now has a national reach through the training of thousands of *Parents as Teachers* parent educators to deliver its home visiting services.

The mission of *Parents as Teachers* is to provide the information, support, and encouragement that parents need to help their children develop optimally during the crucial early years of life. Its goals include increasing parent knowledge of early childhood development and improving parenting practices, providing early detection of developmental delays and health issues, preventing child abuse and neglect, and increasing children's school readiness and school success.

Information about the excellent work of *Parents as Teachers* and the location of the program nearest to you can be obtained from the website of the *Parents as Teachers National Center,* www.parentsasteachers.org.

Parenting coaching. This is also a one-on-one method for learning how to be a more effective parent. It is often done over the Internet and/or the telephone.

Parenting coaching over the Internet involves being linked to a trained coach who is usually a professional from the field of clinical social work, counseling, education, or psychology. The coach relates to you through e-mailing, text messaging, and live chatting. This service focuses on your parenting needs at this particular time in your family's life.

In addition to the individual coaching they provide, these coaches can also inform you about valuable books, videos, DVDs, and community services. Because of the backgrounds and training of the individuals who become parenting coaches, their services are generally considered to be a combination of family education and family counseling.

You will be able to find online and telephone parenting coaches through the *Parent Coaching Institute* at www. parentcoachinginstitute.com.

Now let's learn more about what you can expect when you enroll in some of the parenting and family skill-building programs that have been mentioned.

Parenting Skill-Building Program Descriptions

Here is a sampling of some of the best parenting and family skill-building programs that are available. Let's begin with the program that started the modern skill-building approach to parenting education.

Parent Effectiveness Training (PET)

Program Philosophy

Dr. Thomas Gordon's *PET* program imparts a philosophy of human relationships and a set of child-rearing skills that are intended to assist parents in building warm, close, and enjoyable relationships with their children and in fostering a family environment that is supportive of the needs and growth of each family member. It is based on the philosophy that maximum growth occurs within relationships that are characterized by high degrees of acceptance and genuineness. Acceptance entails being nonjudgmental, and genuineness entails being honestly self-disclosing. Being genuine or real also means revealing when you are feeling judgmental and unaccepting.

PET translates these ideas into a philosophy of parenthood that defines genuine or real parents as those who do not hide their true feelings, who feel both accepting and unaccepting toward their children, who feel different degrees of acceptance toward different children, and who have different attitudes toward the same behaviors of their children at different times.

They accept that their partners in parenting their children are real persons with similarly varied feelings toward their children.

PET believes that the use of physical and psychological power in parent-child relationships contribute to dehumanization and alienation. These values get translated into an injunction against the use of parental power, which means being very careful and judicious in using rewards and punishments in managing the behaviors of their children.

PET also considers that children possess civil rights. This means that children have rights to hold and express feelings and viewpoints and are entitled to their own values, beliefs, preferences, styles, and philosophies of life. *PET* cautions against intruding into those spheres of children's lives that do not have tangible or concrete effects on parents.

Based on these assumptions and values, an effective parent, according to *PET*, would be genuine, self-disclosing, fallible, accepting, and respectful of the feelings, ideas, and values of spouses and children.

The effective parent would also be fair, using influence or persuasion rather than power (rewards and punishments) to get his/her personal needs met. The fairness value implies the involvement of all family members, including children, in decisions that influence them and therefore involves a democratic framework for decision-making. Not using punishment also implies that an effective parent is nonviolent and does not use corporal punishment.

Parenting Strategies and Skills

The *PET* program begins by teaching parents to understand their child's behavior as being either acceptable or unacceptable based on the changing moods and needs of the parent and the child and based on the changing characteristics of the environment. It teaches a method of problem ownership that shows parents how to identify when (1) their child's behaviors are acceptable to the parents but the child indicates that he or she is experiencing a problem in living; (2) their child's behaviors evoke feelings of unacceptance in the parents, which indicates that the parents have a problem; and (3) the child's behaviors are acceptable and no one has a problem.

Active Listening

PET teaches therapeutic listening skills to use when the child is experiencing a problem—a "language of acceptance," or active listening.

To listen actively, parents need to be sensitive and articulate about their children's feeling state, and *PET* also teaches parents how to identify what their children are feeling. Parents need to empathize with their children's problems as they actively listen. An example would be when a child remarks about not being allowed to play ("I never get a chance to get the ball when the bigger kids start playing catch."). The parent actively listens and responds by saying, "You want to play too, and you feel it is not fair for them to leave you out." This usually stimulates a longer conversation in which the actively listening parent frequently uses this communication technique to help the child find a solution to the problem. There are many subtleties and nuances in how and when to listen actively, and the *PET* program presents a variety of options, examples, and pitfalls.

Confrontive I-Messages

PET teaches confrontive communication skills to use when the child's behavior is creating a problem for the parent— Confrontive I-Messages. In delivering these messages, parents

1. describe the unacceptable behavior without blaming,

2. disclose their feelings about the child's behavior, and

3. indicate the tangible effect that the child's behavior is having on them.

These are highly individualized messages that alert the child to attend to and consider the parent's needs. Examples of *Confrontive I-Messages* include the following:

"I'm feeling frustrated and angry because I cannot rest when someone is crawling on my lap."

"I sure get discouraged when I see my clean kitchen dirty again, and I don't want to spend more of my time cleaning it."

To a six-year-old who hit the baby on the head, "Bryant, I get scared to death when the baby is hit on the head! I would sure hate to see him hurt badly. And I get really mad when I see someone big hurting someone a lot smaller. I was so afraid that his little head was going to bleed."

There are also many varieties of I-Messages and subtleties of usage.

Positive I-Messages

PET also teaches parents to use I-Messages when they are spontaneously expressing positive feelings to the child. This is another skill, like effective praise and encouragement, that can be used if you are trying to turn around errors of being unkind in your communications with your children.

Examples of these *Positive I-Messages* include when a child phones to say he has stopped at a friend's house after school, and the parent says, "When you let me know where you are, I feel relieved because then I don't worry about you." Or a child may surprise a parent by cleaning up the kitchen after a snack, and the parent says, "When the kitchen was cleaned up as I started to fix dinner tonight, I appreciated it because I didn't have to spend time cleaning it myself."

Environmental Modification

The program also teaches parents a set of *environmental modification* and childproofing strategies to reduce the likelihood that a child's behavior will create problems. These strategies are called adding, removing, changing the environment, and planning.

When the child's behavior is unacceptable to the parent and an accurate application of *Confrontive I-Messages* or *environmental modification* doesn't work to change the child's behavior, the relationship between the child and the parent now has a problem. Relationship problems are conflicts. These conflicts are inevitable aspects of family life and can either strengthen or destroy a family, depending upon how they are resolved.

Two types of conflicts are identified: conflicts of needs, where the child's needs have tangible and concrete effects on the parent, and conflicts of values, where the child's needs do not have such effects or where the child doesn't "buy" the effects that the parent says he or she is experiencing. Parents are taught to distinguish between the two types of conflicts and to utilize different methods in dealing with them.

The No-Lose Conflict Resolution Method

When conflicts of needs exist, parents are taught systematic and democratic negotiation skills for resolving them without having to resort to parental power—the no-lose conflict resolution method. Examples of conflicts of needs are the following:

- When the child doesn't help with the dishes and instead starts reading a book in preparation for an upcoming school exam

- The child leaves the parents' tools on the front sidewalk, and the parent is afraid they will be stolen

- The child continues to play baseball in a next-door lot even though he has been told that the family must go somewhere in an hour

- A child continues to stop and gaze in store windows after the parent has indicated that there is reason to rush

The program indicates that most parents deal with these conflicts in a win-lose fashion. Either the parent gives in and loses and the child wins (a permissive parent) or the parent uses power and wins and the child loses (an authoritarian parent).

The *no-lose conflict resolution method* is an alternative to this win-lose approach. This method enlists the ideas and viewpoints of the child in arriving at mutually agreeable solutions. It is clearly more time-consuming than the win-lose approach. It consists of six interrelated processes:

1. Identifying and defining the conflicting needs

2. Generating possible alternative solutions

3. Evaluating the alternative solutions

4. Deciding on the best acceptable solution

5. Working out ways of implementing the solution

6. Following up to evaluate how well it worked

This method interrelates with the other *PET* methods. For example, during a conflict resolution sequence, the parent often must shift gears and employ I-Messages and active listening in order to facilitate arriving at an acceptable solution. Parents are also taught to use this method to help others resolve conflicts, such as helping two children resolve conflicts by using this method in a facilitator or consultant capacity.

Conflicts of values exist when parents feel unaccepting toward a child's behavior and the child doesn't believe that the behavior tangibly affects the parents or that the behavior is bad for him or her.

Examples of values conflicts include when children swear and the parents find this unacceptable; when children choose friends, clothing, or hairstyles that parents find unacceptable; when children stop wanting to go to church; and so forth. At such junctions, the program orients parents to own the problem and either model, consult, or modify themselves.

Within the *PET* program, modeling refers to engaging in behaviors that are consistent with the values you would like to see in your child (e.g., not swearing). Consulting refers to giving information or offering opinions but not preaching or demanding that the child change.

Modifying self includes a close examination of one's values, with the possibility of the parent accepting the child's values.

This classic and pioneering skill-building program is usually taught in eight three-hour sessions by a highly trained instructor whose roles include being a facilitator of learning, a skill model, and a course manager rather than a therapist.

There is also a self-study or self-taught version available that enables parents to learn *PET* skills at home on their own or with a spouse or other partner. It is called *Family Effectiveness Training*. The program is led by Dr. Gordon. It provides eighteen to twenty hours of study and practice, using video and audiotapes and study and resource guides.

Further information about *PET* can be obtained from Gordon Training International: www.gordontraining.com.

Learning this parenting skill-building program is learning a multiyear positive parenting style.

CICC's Trio of Parenting Skill-Building Programs

Here, you will learn more about the three-parenting skill-building programs created by the Center for the Improvement of Child Caring (CICC), which is the parent education organization I founded in 1974. The three are the *New Confident Parenting*, the *Effective Black Parenting*, and the *Los Niños Bien Educados* programs.

These programs are designed for use with all parents, regardless of the age of the child and regardless of whether the children do or do not have special needs. The programs teach a positive parenting philosophy (the social learning philosophy) and a series of very practical parenting skills to enhance the quality of family life and to decrease child behavior problems. The social learning philosophy is reflected in the basic assumption that all parenting practices are learned, and therefore, new practices can not only be learned at any time but old ones can be unlearned.

The *Effective Black Parenting* and *Los Niños Bien Educados* programs are culturally adapted versions of the *Confident Parenting* program. These are the first culturally adapted parenting skill-building programs in the nation. They teach a similar positive philosophy and teach all the skills that are taught in *Confident Parenting*. In addition, they teach the skills in a culturally sensitive manner, they frame the teaching of the skills within the values and histories of each of the cultural groups, and they contain additional contents, skills, and topics that address parenting challenges that are unique to each cultural group. In terms of the definition of *parenting* that was shared in an earlier section, these two programs address how parents enculturate their children to the values and life circumstances of their culture.

Learning any of the three CICC programs is learning a multiyear positive parenting style.

The New Confident Parenting Program

Parents often feel controlled by their children's misbehavior because they do not know how to set limits effectively. We may pay so much attention when our children misbehave that we forget to notice the cooperative and peaceful times.

The *New Confident Parenting* program teaches parents how to pay attention to and increase the times when their children's behavior is good.

It also teaches effective limit-setting skills so that parents will not feel victimized by their children's misbehavior.

The program begins by teaching parents that behavior is shaped by its consequences. Here, a good deal of emphasis is placed on helping parents transform global descriptions of children's functioning ("he's selfish," for example) into specific behavioral descriptions ("he doesn't share his toys with his brother").

Parents are then taught exactly how to pinpoint the specific behaviors that they would like to see their children engage in more frequently and those they would like to see less of. This pinpointing involves not only being specific about observable behaviors but also indicating where and when the parent would like to see the behavior (at bedtime, in the morning, at the dinner table, and so on).

Parents are then advised about various procedures for counting and charting specific behaviors so they have a record of what is taking place. This record serves as a standard against which the effectiveness of the parenting skills or methods that are taught in the *Confident Parenting* program can be judged, as the methods are designed to increase or decrease specific behaviors. Thus, the charting of behaviors can be used to see whether a method is working.

Through a combination of instructor presentations and demonstrations and parental role-playing and home assignments, parents are taught exactly how to use the program's various skills to bring out more of their children's positive and appropriate behaviors and to decrease their negative or inappropriate actions.

The program is designed for maximum flexibility in both the length and content of the program. It is based on the fifteen instructional units that are available in its parent's handbook.

It is also based upon, or can be supplemented with, a DVD entitled *Yelling, Threatening and Putting Down: What to Do Instead.* The DVD has four segments that depict parents from different ethnic groups coping with typical child-rearing challenges and learning to use a variety of parenting skills and strategies.

The units of instructions are described in the parent's handbook, including a unit we have already been exposed to—effective praising—or as it is called in the program, *behavior-specific praise*. Most units are accompanied by homework practice exercises.

For a specific class in this program, all fifteen units of instruction can be used or only some of the units. That decision can be made by the sponsoring agency or by the instructor. It also could be made with consultation from the parents who are to be in the actual class.

Short of running a class that covers all fifteen units, an alternative would be to conduct a shorter class that focuses on the management of child-behavior problems, like disruptiveness, fears, shyness, tantrums, and disobedience. Here, the class would consist of the units "Learning through Consequences," "Behavior-Specific Praise," "Mild Social Disapproval," "Ignoring, Time-Out," and "Special Incentives." Another option would be to run a longer class by adding the units on "Modeling," "Family Rules," and the "Thinking Parent's Strategy."

A one-day seminar version can also be run. Here, the specific units of instruction can include any four or five of the units.

For these options, the same parent handbook is supplied to the parents. This enables the parents to follow the units in their class or seminar, as well as to become familiar with the entire program.

All versions also involve the use of relevant charts and drawings and the use of the *family rule cards* if the family rule units of instruction are to be taught.

In terms of the use of the DVD *Yelling, Threatening and Putting Down: What to Do Instead*, there are also several options. It can be decided to utilize the entire DVD with its four segments and its four cultural groups or just use specific segments from the DVD. The entire DVD or its separate segments can be used as a supplement to the instructional units. The DVD could also be conducted as a separate parenting program. It has its own leader's guide.

Units of Instruction

The fifteen instructional units that can be taught are the following:

1. *Welcome and Introduction*

   The Confident Parenting Approach

   The Needs and Rights of Children and Parents

2. *Why Do Kids Do What They Do?*

   Learning through Modeling

   Learning through Consequences

3. *Social Rewards: The Art of Effective Praising*

   Expecting Too Much Too Soon

   The Personal Touch

   The Advantages of Social Rewards

   How to Socially Reward

   Putting It All Together

Basic Components of Ignoring

This method is also a way of decreasing child misbehavior. It involves ignoring or withdrawing attention. The essence of this skill is that it must be used consistently in response to the behaviors that it seeks to reduce. It is best used the first time a child engages in a new inappropriate behavior, such as swearing, and with annoying behaviors, such as persistently asking for cookies or interrupting while the parent is on the phone or talking with someone else.

It consists of five behavioral components:

1. Looking away from the child

2. Moving away from the child

3. Neutral facial expression

4. Ignoring the child's verbalizations

5. Ignoring immediately upon noticing the problematic behavior

9. *Time-Out from Parental Attention*

Punishment: Pros and Cons

Time-Out: A Gentle but Consistent Form of Discipline

The Rationale for Time-Out

A Special Rule When Using Time-Out

How to Use Time-Out

This skill is a form of punishment that is used when all else fails and the child's behavior has exceeded reasonable limits. It refers to time-out from social interaction and attention. *Time-out* is explained to the child as going to a cooling-off place for a short period of time when her/his behavior has gone too far.

Parents are instructed to make a rule about how time-out is to be used. For example, the parents may articulate a family rule about how disagreements are to be handled. (We *do* tell each other what our opinions and feelings are. We *don't* hit each other.) The child is informed that when he or she breaks this family rule, time-out will be used. Then, when the child breaks the rule, the parents begin and follow through on the time-out sequence:

1. Remain calm.

2. State the rule and its consequence.

3. Ignore the child's extraneous verbalizations and excuses.

4. Follow through quickly by initiating the time-out procedure.

Soon after the child is removed from time-out and when he/she is behaving appropriately again, parents are instructed to praise the child to show that they still love him or her and that they do not hold grudges.

Practice Using the Method

Choose a Suitable Time-Out Area

10.   *Special Incentive System*

Here, parents are taught how to design and implement a special incentive system. In this system, the child earns points, stars, or tokens for engaging in specified desirable behaviors (the "do sides" of various family rules). The child turns these points in for various tangible rewards and/or special privileges. The rewards or privileges are chosen from a reward menu that is negotiated cooperatively by the parent and the child.

Initiating this system also involves creating charts where parents can keep track of the points that a child earns each day for engaging in the "do side" behaviors that the parent wants to see more of. Here is an example of such a chart:

BEHAVIOR	S	M	T	W	TH	F	S
1. CLOTHES PUT AWAY							
2. TOYS PUT AWAY							
3. BOOKS PUT AWAY							
4. BED MADE							
TOTAL POINTS							
POINTS SPENT							
POINTS SAVED							

The components of a special incentive system are

1. *defining* desirable behavior,

2. *counting* the target behavior(s),

3. *creating* the reward menu,

4. *establishing* the exchange ratio (i.e., how many points earn which rewards),

5. *charting* behaviors,

6. *praise* for positive behavioral changes,

7. *program adjustments*, and

8. *phasing out* the program.

The Anatomy of a Special Incentive Program

The Case of Alan M.: From a Slob to a Saint in Several Weeks

Contracting—An exercise in give-and-take where a contract is made between teens and parents where each agrees to do or not do something ("I will have my room cleaned each week on Saturday") in exchange for the other also agreeing to do or not do something ("I will not nag you about the friends you keep").

A Note to Parents on Attitude

The DVD on Yelling, Threatening and Putting Down

What to Do Instead

There are four excellent, professionally acted segments on this DVD. Each presents a parenting challenge for which the parents in the DVD lose their composure and begin to yell, threaten, or put their children down.

Then the DVD is stopped, and the instructor asks, "What would you do instead?" The class discusses their ideas. Then the DVD is started again, and it shows some excellent ways of dealing with the challenges. Many of the ways that are demonstrated involve the use of the skills and strategies from the *Confident Parenting Program*.

Segment One: When Children Are Very Active, with a White Family

A father arrives home from work tired, but he must watch after his two-year-old son as his wife has an evening appointment. He starts to watch a basketball game. His son starts to seek his attention by bringing a bucket of toys in front of the TV screen and making a lot of noise. The father gets frustrated and yells at the child to stop interrupting the game and making so much noise.

Techniques Demonstrated to Deal with the Situation

> Think <u>before</u> you act.
> Talk to your spouse or another parent to understand your child.
> Think about the causes of your child's behavior.
> Enjoy your child's energy level and let him know it.
> Redirect your child to a calmer activity.
> Combine your need and your child's need.

Segment Two: When Children Get Angry, with an African American Family

A mother of a six-year-old notices that the child has begun throwing blocks around because the tower she was trying to make keeps falling. The mother tells her to stop throwing around the blocks. When the child continues to throw them, the mother threatens to take away the blocks and never return them.

Techniques Demonstrated to Deal with the Situation

Recognize when your child's frustration is rising and intervene <u>before</u> things start flying.

Think of family rules as a two-sided coin with a *do* side and a *don't* side. Emphasize the *do* side rather than the *don't* side.

Acknowledge and manage your own anger.

Model the desired behavior: stay calm, help your child, and talk her through the activity.

Empathize with your child and let her know you understand her feelings.

Keep a sense of humor.

Praise your child when she plays calmly.

Encourage your child to express her feelings in words, and listen to her response.

Redirect your child to a less frustrating activity.

If your child continues throwing, remind her firmly and calmly of the rules.

Give her a choice that is logically related to the behavior. Follow through.

Do not get into power struggles over every little thing.

Have fun together and show her you love her.

Segment Three: When Children Whine, with a Latino Family

A mother is shopping in a market with her seven-year-old daughter. The daughter wants her to get some special items for dessert and presses her mother by saying, "Daddy always buys those candies." The mother, who sees other customers watching their interaction, finally caves in, throws the candy in the shopping cart, and puts her daughter down, saying, "I can't stand you. You're such a little pain!"

Techniques to Use to Deal with the Situation

Have a family meeting, discuss the issue, and agree to one set of rules.

Calmly and clearly communicate expectations to your child in advance.

Help your child practice the desired behavior ahead of time.

Give your child a snack before entering a supermarket.

Give your child a job to do in the store and praise her when she is helpful.

Be firm: do not encourage whining by wishy-washy statements or by whining yourself.

Consider rewarding your child at the end of a shopping trip if she has acted appropriately.

Follow through firmly and calmly with the rules and expectations you have established.

Segment Four: When Siblings Fight, with an Asian American Family

A father is working at the dining room table at home. His eight-year-old daughter and twelve-year-old son are arguing about the use of a CD. Their fighting escalates, with kicking and name-calling. Dad steps in and attempts to figure out who started the fight but gets exasperated and yells at the children.

The children settle down, but only for a moment. Soon the fighting starts again, and Dad blows up. He yells at them and threatens, "If you two don't knock it off, you're both grounded!" And puts them down, "I don't believe what babies you guys are!"

Techniques to Use in Dealing with This Situation

Hold a family meeting. Have everyone take turns listening and talking. As a parent, acknowledge any part you may have in a pattern of family fighting.

Agree upon rules for peacefully solving disagreements. The rules should be specific as to what behaviors are desirable. Write the rules and post them so they are easy to see.

Set a positive example of peaceful conflict resolution.

Learn to distinguish between different levels of conflict: if it is a minor disagreement, ignore it and let the children work it out.

If it is squabbling that is getting out of control, with name-calling, hitting, kicking, etc., stop the fighting and remove the object of disagreement.

If it is fighting that is already out of control, with abusive language or violence, separate the children. Remind them that insults and physical attaches are not allowed. Have them go to separate areas to cool off.

Help the children learn to solve problems without violence. Explain that they need to use appropriate language, listen without interrupting, and reach a solution acceptable to everyone concerned.

If the children have difficulty solving the problem, help them. Your goal should not be to settle the disagreement, but to help them to learn how to settle it themselves. Do not impose your own solution unless they obviously cannot reach an agreement.

Listen to the children's ideas. Suggest a few of your own. Write the ideas down.

Have patience and remain impartial and fair.

The parent handbook and the DVD on *Yelling, Threatening and Putting Down: What to Do Instead* can be obtained from the CICC website, www.ciccparenting.org. When there, click on Shop/Books and then on the *New Confident Parenting Program.*

Effective Black Parenting Program

Raising African American children in the United States is an extremely challenging task. Although all children progress through similar stages of development and all children need nurturance and sensitive guidance, African American children and their parents face special problems because of our country's history of racism and discrimination. These problems often make it harder to raise proud and capable African American children.

Until CICC created the *Effective Black Parenting* program (*EBPP*) in the late 1970s, there were no skill-building programs that addressed these problems head-on. There were also no programs that taught parenting skills in a manner that was respectful of African American patterns of communication and that recognized the African roots of the extended black family. Thus, the program occupies a very special place in the history of parenting education in the United States.

EBPP provides an excellent learning and relearning context to help parents of African American children do the best job possible. Its basic ideas are derived from the writings of African American parenting scholars, from research with African American parents, and from adaptations of *Confident Parenting* skills.

The research that was conducted to help inform what is taught in the program showed that (1) the parents had very high expectations for their children's achievement, (2) most of the parents used harsh disciplinary practices that originated historically as survival adjustments to slavery, and (3) less than half of the parents shared positive aspects of their culture with their children, and many made disparaging comments about their culture and heritage.

These findings were used as a basis for creating new instructional units about cultural issues that could be taught along with the skills from the *Confident Parenting* program.

The new instructional units included an achievement strategy for raising African American children— "the path to the pyramid of success for black children."

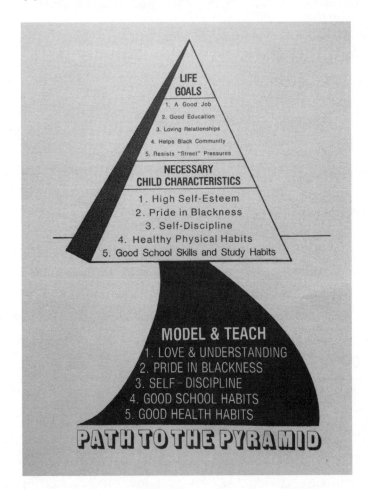

As can be seen in the drawing that is used in the program, this strategy links the life goals that parents have for their children with the characteristics the children need to develop to achieve those life goals. It then informs parents what they need to do to maximize the chances of their children developing these characteristics (i.e., what they need to model and teach their children).

The important life goals are generated through engaging the parents in a call-and-response exercise like those used in many African American churches. Because the pyramids that most people are aware of were constructed in Egypt and Egypt is part of the continent of Africa, parents are informed that their people created the major pyramids. This is one of the ways that the program promotes pride in the African heritage (pride in blackness).

Parents are further informed that the parenting strategies, skills, and topics that are taught in the program are designed to keep the parents and the children on that path.

The parenting skills that are taught in the program are the following:

> Describing and Counting Behaviors
>
> Effective Praise
>
> Mild Social Disapproval
>
> Systematic Ignoring
>
> Time-Out from Social Attention
>
> The Point-System Method
>
> Chitchat Time

In addition to "the path to the pyramid of success for black children" strategy, "a traditional black discipline versus modern black self-discipline" and "a pride in blackness" strategy are also taught.

Other parenting strategies and topics are also taught and covered, including the following:

> Family Rule Guidelines
>
> The Thinking Parent's Approach
>
> Children's Developing Abilities
>
> Drugs and Our Children
>
> Single Parenting

Each of the parenting strategies and skills in EBPP is taught by referring to African proverbs such as "Children are the reward of life" and "A shepherd does not strike his sheep." The systematic use of these proverbs helps to ground the teachings of the program in the wisdom and skillfulness of the African ancestors. Their use is another example of the ways that the program promotes cultural pride.

The complete program is taught in fifteen three-hour class sessions, with the last session also serving as a graduation celebration. This program also has a briefer version that is taught through a one-day seminar structure.

Here is another example of the program's culturally specific strategies regarding the teaching of the difference between *traditional black discipline versus modern black self-discipline*. This has turned out to be one of the most influential of all features of this national model program. It is taught in the fourth session. The previous sessions had taught the pyramid of success, the counting of behaviors, and the effective-praise skill.

The session includes an exercise from the program's research to explore their meanings of the concept of disciplining children by asking for their word associations to that process. Then they are shown the responses of the African American parents who were part of the research study. Their associations reflected an appreciation for disciplining children that consisted greatly of the use of harsh consequences such as whipping, hitting, spanking, and verbal chastisement as the primary methods for gaining child cooperation and obedience.

The instructor then provides some historical perspective on this "traditional black discipline" orientation. Quoting from African American scholars on parenting and using descriptions from the whipping-in-front-of-all-the-slaves scene from the original *Roots* television show, the instructor conveys that this approach was developed in response to the demands of slavery and more recent periods of racial discrimination. The traditional approach responds to the need for survival in a hostile world where opportunities for advancement are limited and where the consequences of violating social role expectations were severe (e.g., imprisonment, brutal physical assault, death).

The instructor indicates that the primary goal of this approach is to ensure the child's survival and reduce the risks of the undesirable social consequences by raising respectful black children who do not question authority.

The instructor contrasts this approach with modern black self-discipline, which is based on positive, self-directed, achievement-oriented approaches. Here, discipline is designed to enhance self-esteem, self-confidence, and feelings of personal and collective competence. This approach to black parenting evolved during the civil rights and black power movements.

The parents are then informed that in the modern approach, positive-consequence methods such as effective praise are disciplinary methods. They are further advised that the use of clear family rules and reasons for rules, along with the frequent use of positive consequences, reduces the need for corrective consequences such as punishment, spanking, and whipping.

The full spectrum of parenting methods that the program teaches is introduced at this point in the program, and parents see that they are consistent with the more modern approach. They are also introduced to the proverb "a shepherd does not strike his sheep" and to the idea of "appealing to their minds and not their behinds" in considering how to discipline their children.

EBPP has become the program of choice for hundreds of institutions nationwide that serve African Americans. These institutions have different missions. Some are institutions whose missions are substance-abuse prevention, child-abuse prevention, delinquency prevention, and school reform. Thus, nearly every type of health and human service, educational, and faith group has found *EBPP* worthwhile.

You can find several videos about the impact of this program in the page on CICC's website (www.ciccparenting.org) entitled Videos and Photos. The parent's handbook and a book of interviews of parents who have completed the program (*The Soulful Parent* book) can be found by going to the Shop/Books page.

Los Niños Bien Educados Program

Developed especially for Spanish-speaking and Latino-origin parents, the *Los Niños Bien Educados Program (LNBE)* is respectful of the unique traditions and customs of families of Latino descent. The program is particularly sensitive to the variety of adjustments that are made as such families acculturate to life in the United States.

The program is built around the traditional Latino family value of raising children to be *bien educados* (i.e., well-behaved, in a social and personal sense and well educated in an academic sense). This includes, in general, knowing one's place in the family and being respectful of adults and elders. However, because of the variety of countries from which parents of Latino descent come and because some are newly emigrated, while others have been part of the United States for generations, the program does not assume that all parents of Latino descent have the same definition of *bien educados*. Thus, the program begins by exploring parental definitions of the term *bien educados*.

These definitions are usually of a very general nature, such as saying that it means being well-mannered, well-behaved, respectful, and so forth. The parents are then asked to provide specific examples of the behaviors that they consider to be reflective of a child who is well-mannered (bien educados). They also explore their definitions of a child who is behaving in a *mal educados* fashion. The program mentions that all children sometimes behave in such a fashion.

From these basic cultural groundings and definitions, *LNBE* looks at how these definitions are expressed in the traditional family, gender role, and age expectations of children. Then it teaches parents a wide variety of strategies and skills for promoting and maintaining those child behaviors that they define as constituting bien educados and for reducing those that they see as reflecting mal educados.

As part of the program, parents are oriented to consider the potential causes of mal educados.

Parents are also taught basic child development to assist them in arriving at age-appropriate expectations. Information about child abuse and child-abuse laws helps broaden understandings of what is considered proper and improper parental behavior in the United States.

This program also addresses important cultural issues having to do with the different types of adjustments that families of Latino descent make to the United States and the impact of traditional family and gender roles on the expectations that parents have for their children.

All skills are taught with the use of *dichos*, or Spanish sayings, to help nest them in a culturally and linguistically familiar context. Amusing drawings, like that of Maria and Mateo above, also enliven the teaching of skills and concepts. All sessions end with a *platica* or chat, where parents take leadership roles in solving common problems.

Here is a listing of the parenting strategies, skills, and topics covered in the complete program:

- *Culturally Specific Parenting Strategies*

    Defining Bien and Mal Educados

    Traditional Family and Gender Roles

    Adjusting and Acculturating to the United States

- *General Parenting Strategies*

    Social Learning Ideas and Pinpointing and Counting Behavior

    Parental Functions and Responsibilities

    Family Expectations Are Like a Coin and Family Expectation Guidelines

    The Causes of Child Behavior and Considering the Causes Before and After You Act

In the *LNBE program*, it was decided to refer to family rules as family expectations. It was thought that using the term *expectations* (or in Spanish, *expectativas*) was closer to how most Latino parents think about what they want their children to do and not to do.

In both the *Confident Parenting* and *Effective Black Parenting programs*, this same drawing is called *Family Rules Are Like a Coin* as these large populations are believed to be more comfortable with the concept of rules. For all groups, the drawing assists parents in deciding which type of skill to employ in response to whether the child is engaging in a *do-* or *don't-side* behavior. For example, parents are oriented to respond to their children's *do-side* behaviors with a skill like effective praise and to respond to *don't-side* actions with skills like time-out, disapproval, or ignoring.

Basic Parenting Skills Taught in a Culturally Sensitive Manner, Using Latino American Language Expressions and Dichos

Effective Praise

Mild Social Disapproval

Systematic Ignoring

Time-Out from Attention

The Point System (Special Incentives)

First/Then (First You Work, Then You Play)

Show and Tell (Modeling and Demonstrating Bien Educados' Behaviors)

Family Chat or *Platica* (e.g., regarding family changes in schedules)

Special Topical Coverage

Child Abuse Laws and Proper Parenting

The program is designed to be taught in Spanish or English and consists of twelve three-hour training sessions, the last of which includes a graduation ceremony. Like all the CICC programs, this one also can be taught as a one-day seminar version. The parent handbook, in English or Spanish, can be obtained in the Shop/Books section of the CICC website: www.ciccparenting.org. Videos of news shows on the program can be viewed on the Videos/Photo section of the website.

Positive Indian Parenting Program

This unique parenting program was developed by the National Indian Child Welfare Institute. Its subtitle, *Honoring Our Children by Honoring Our Traditions*, highlights the fact that it draws on traditional American Indian child-rearing to help contemporary Indian parents approach their children in a very positive and culturally knowledgeable way. The developers relied heavily on consultation with tribal elders, Indian professionals, and parents in evolving this eight-session program.

The developers note the tremendous tribal and regional diversity of the American Indian population, with more than five hundred federally recognized tribes or bands. Each of these groups has its own child-rearing patterns, value systems, communication patterns, and behaviors.

Despite this rich diversity, the program developers believe that there are at least three major traditions that are common to most, if not all, American Indians: the oral tradition (or storytelling), the spiritual nature of child rearing, and the role of the extended family.

As for the oral tradition, they explain that "through the telling of stories and legends, children learned about proper relationships with other people and the environment. They were taught to be good observers and to understand the meaning of nonverbal communication."

The spiritual nature of child-rearing was evident in the belief held by some tribes that children were special gifts from the Creator. The tribal elders used praise and reassurance to encourage positive and loving relationships between parents and their children. Prophecies were often made about the worth of the child and his or her future.

The whole community recognized a child's growth and development through rites-of-passage ceremonies. These ceremonies were important for the children too. The naming ceremony, for example, helped a child establish his or her identity in the tribe.

The extended family was the major socializer of children. Individuals lived in small communities where they relied on each other for survival, and children learned quickly how important it was to cooperate, share, and show respect for elders.

The consequences of breaking the community's rules or limits were clearly understood and accepted. Discipline was carefully tailored to make the child understand a specific rule or limit.

Nurturing was an important part of traditional child-rearing. The use of cradleboards, for example, meant that infants were rarely separated from their mothers. However, no one person carried the whole burden of raising a child. Grandparents, aunts and uncles, and cousins were always nearby to help when parents had other responsibilities. Sometimes, extended family members had specific roles to play, e.g., grandfather the storyteller, uncle the disciplinarian.

These are the old ways—ways that existed prior to white influence. The program developers assert that the white influence, through such institutions as boarding schools, not only stripped away cultural traditions but instilled a "spare the rod and spoil the child" philosophy that runs against the traditional American Indian nurturing approach to children. It is out of a dual desire to reclaim traditional modes of child-rearing and to abandon the "spare the rod" approach that this program was created.

The topics covered in the eight sessions are "Traditional Parenting," "Lessons of the Storyteller," "Lessons of the Cradleboard," "Harmony in Child-Rearing," "Traditional Behavior Management," "Lessons of Mother Nature," "Praise in Traditional Parenting," and "Choices in Parenting."

Further information about *Positive Indian Parenting* can be obtained from here:

National Indian Child Welfare Association

5100 SW Macadam, Suite 300

Portland, OR 97239

(503) 222-4044

www.nicwa.org

NICWA's home page has a stunning video about the prior and current treatment of Indian children in America. It should be watched by everyone.

Siblings Without Rivalry

This six-session, topic-centered program by Adele Faber and Elaine Mazlish is devoted entirely to addressing the inevitable rivalries and conflicts of siblings. It provides unique perspectives on these rivalries and a variety of creative ways to help parents manage them.

Session One: Helping Siblings Deal with Their Feelings about One Another

What would it feel like to have one's spouse bring home another wife or husband and expect you to immediately love the intruder?

This stunning analogy serves as a vehicle for helping parents appreciate the conflicted and powerful feelings children have for their siblings.

They are also asked to recall their feelings for their own siblings.

A variety of ways are introduced for helping their children deal with negative feelings about a sibling, including acknowledging those feelings ("You feel he does it to irritate you" or "You don't like my spending so much time with her") rather than dismissing them. The program also helps children channel their feelings into symbolic or creative outlets ("No hurting your sister! You can show me your feelings with your doll") or, for an older child, "I think your sister needs to know in writing how enraged you are!"

Session Two: Keeping Children Separate and Unequal

Parents learn how children react to being compared unfavorably or favorably and how siblings feel about being treated equally. Ways to treat children unequally and still be fair are modeled and taught. Parents focus on each child's individual needs instead of worrying about giving equal amounts. Also included are techniques for showing children how they are loved uniquely ("No one has your thoughts, your feelings, and your smile. I'm so glad you're my daughter!") instead of claiming equal love.

Session Three: Siblings in Roles

This session shows why brothers and sisters are often cast, and cast each other, into different roles and how powerful these roles affect their relationships with each other. Skills to help free each child to become his or her whole self are taught, such as how a parent helps a child who has been cast in the role of the victim to stand up for herself ("You can tell your brother 'Daddy bought it for me. It's mine. I decide if I want to share!'") or how a parent teaches a child who is a bully that he's capable of civil action ("No clobbering! You know how to get what you want without using physical force").

Session Four: When the Kids Fight

This session deals with the inevitable and sometimes dangerous impulse for siblings to fight each other. A step-by-step procedure to help children work out their problems themselves is suggested. Parents learn other skills to use when their children fight over property and when the fighting is heading toward hurting. Thus, a series of interventions are offered for parents to use, depending on the dangerousness of the conflict. The tactic of last resort, as in other programs such as *Confident Parenting*, is separation or time-out.

Session Five: Problem-Solving

Here, a multistep approach is presented for helping children deal with problems they can't work out themselves. It enables parents to sit down with their young combatants and help them move toward a way to resolve their conflicts by writing down each child's feelings and concerns without comment, then reading them aloud. The parents acknowledge the difficulty of the problem and ask everyone to come up with ways to solve the problem. Then all parties review each suggestion together and check those to which everyone can agree, shaking hands over the agreements and making plans to meet again.

Session Six: A Final Review

The last session is used to review and consolidate the skills learned. It includes applying all the skills in potentially explosive situations.

Finally, parents are given a second opportunity to look at their own sibling relationships and to see those relationships from the new perspectives they have gained through the program.

More information about *Siblings Without Rivalry* can be obtained from the website of the authors: www. fabermazlish.com.

The Nurturing Programs

These programs by Dr. Stephen Bavolek represent age-related, skill-building programs in the versions prepared for parents with different-aged children, as well being family skill-building programs in that all members of the family participate in each version of the program.

The origins of the *Nurturing* programs were very different from those of the other group parenting programs described thus far. They originated as educational interventions for abusive and dysfunctional families. At the time that the initial *Nurturing* program was designed, research with families who were abusive to their babies and young children showed that certain characteristic outlooks of parents in these families tended to contribute to the maltreatment of their children. These included the following:

1. Inappropriate expectations about the abilities of their children, where the parents assumed that their children could accomplish certain tasks long before their bodies and minds had developed sufficiently to accomplish them. The result was that there was always friction and disappointment, and the children were left feeling that they could never satisfy their parents.

2. Lack of awareness of the child's emotional needs and a related inability to respond appropriately. This lack of empathic understanding contributed further to the misunderstanding and poor nurturing of children.

3. Strong belief in the value of using corporal punishment to control and discipline children. Given these parents' misunderstandings of their children's abilities and their own difficulties with empathy, their belief in corporal punishment often got translated into severe beatings to keep children in line.

4. A tendency to expect children to attend to and take care of the needs of the parents. This reversal of the roles of parents and children fueled some serious and even fatal interactions between parents and babies. Here, the baby's incessant crying was interpreted to mean that the baby did not love the parent or where a toddler's developmentally appropriate negativity was deliberately making life miserable for an already overburdened parent.

The originators of the *Nurturing* program chose to teach topics and skills specifically designed to address and counteract these harmful outlooks and attitudes. To counter inappropriate expectations, they included specific information about children's developmental stages and what realistically could be expected from children of different ages and stages.

In response to parental problems with being empathic, they provided skills for recognizing and identifying feelings and methods to expand self-awareness.

To counter strong beliefs in corporal punishment, they provided conceptual tools for distinguishing between discipline and punishment. They also included specific and nonviolent behavior management skills for setting limits on children's behavior. Many of these behavior management skills are like those taught in the *CICC Trio of Programs*.

Throughout the *Nurturing* program, it is reinforced that the parent's main role is that of a nurturer, thus counteracting the tendency to reverse this role.

In addition, the creators of the *Nurturing* program were also aware that many abusive parents were themselves maltreated as children and that they needed to be nurtured or reparented. Thus, special activities were included in the program to help nurture the parents.

The program creators also realized that because the children of these parents were so poorly treated, the children themselves would need special help and training. This led them to design a program for the children to run concurrently with the program for the parents. The result of these ideas is *Nurturing* programs including all family members.

The entire family comes to the class. The parents go into one group, and the children go into their own group. Both learn about nurturing ways of relating to themselves and to their family members. Halfway through the session, the parents and children come back together for some mutual nurturing and training and for snacks and fun activities. Then they return to their individual groups for additional training. They end the session by coming back together for a group hug.

All versions of the program emphasize the nurturing philosophy of developing empathy (the ability to be aware of the needs of others and to value those needs) and about the development of self-esteem (feeling good about themselves as men and women and boys and girls). Each version also teaches a variety of skills to replace the use of corporal punishment.

A creative array of teaching methods is employed, including games, coloring books, videotaped presentations of concepts and skills, scary touch dolls, family logs, and videotapes such as *Shaking, Hitting and Spanking: What to Do Instead* and *Nurturing Touch*, where infant message techniques are demonstrated.

There now exist *Nurturing* programs for parents who are about to become parents (the prenatal program); program versions for parents of very young children, which are available in both English and Spanish; program versions for parents of elementary school-age children and for parents of adolescents; and a program for teenage parents and their families. Here's an example:

Nurturing Program for Parents and Adolescents

The often extraordinary intellectual, physical, and emotional developments that occur during the teenage years are presented and discussed, and specific strategies for relating to teenagers are taught.

Parents are told that two words best summarize the period of adolescence: independence and autonomy. All adolescents, to some degree or another, want to feel in control, want to make their own decisions, want to choose their own friends, and do not want to be told how to look, how to dress, or how to think. In short, adolescents want a piece of the action. They want to be included in making decisions, especially those that directly affect them. The Nurturing program concludes that the key to living with adolescents is to let them exercise some autonomy and independence.

The program informs parents that the adolescent's ability to think abstractly has grown by leaps and bounds. Instead of dealing with things the way they are, adolescents begin to think about things the way they could be. Statements by parents such as "this is my house and as long as you live under my roof, you obey my rules" simply are not accepted by teenagers. They want to know the logic or reasoning behind some action or rule. They do not want to follow a rule just because someone says so. Parents who do not realize the purpose behind all the whys that a teenager asks can find life with their teenager to be one battle after another.

The program stresses that talking with, listening to, compromising, negotiating, and including adolescents as decision makers are the only ways parents and teenagers can live together in harmony.

The program also helps parents and teenagers work together to arrive at livable family rules, with rewards for following rules as well as penalties for violating them. Rewards suggested for desirable, rule-following actions include praise, touch, privileges, allowance, and objects that money can buy. The penalties or punishments include loss of privileges, being grounded, restitution (paying for some misdeed with money or extra chores), and parental disappointment.

Issues such as pregnancy delay, sex, sexuality, HIV/AIDS, suicide, chemical use, and peer pressure are given special coverage. As in all *Nurturing* programs, the youth have their own group in which to discuss these matters independently of their parents, adding opportunities for them to explore and successfully deal with these important issues on their own.

This *Nurturing* program consists of twelve three-hour training sessions.

More can be learned about all the *Nurturing* programs at the website of Family Development Resources: www. nurturingparenting.com.

As is probably obvious, although all the Nurturing programs were initially created for parents who had been maltreating their children, they are quite applicable and useful for all parents who want to do a good job raising their children.

Stop and Think Program

The Stop and Think program by Dr. Howard M. Knoof also teaches parents how to teach their children important skills. The program helps parents teach their children several basic and advanced social skills.

Survival skills. These are the most basic skills that are needed to be successful with all the other skills that are taught. These skills lay the foundation for all other skills and include teaching children how to do the following:

- Listen
- Follow directions
- Use nice talk
- Use brave talk
- Reward themselves
- Evaluate themselves

Interpersonal skills. These skills help children interact successfully and get along with siblings, peers, older and younger students, parents, teachers, and other adults. Included here are the following:

- Sharing

- Asking for permission

- Joining an activity

- Contributing to discussions

- Answering questions

- How to interrupt

- How to wait your turn

- How to wait for an adult's attention

- Beginning/ending a conversation

- Giving/accepting compliments

Problem-solving skills. These skills help children solve or prevent individual, interactive, peer, or classroom problems, and these include the following:

- Asking for help

- Apologizing

- Accepting consequences

- Setting a goal

- Deciding what to do

- Avoiding trouble

- Understanding the feelings of others

- Responding to failure

Conflict resolution skills. These help children deal with highly emotional situations and resolve existing intrapersonal and interpersonal conflicts. Included here are the following:

- Dealing with teasing

- Dealing with losing

- Dealing with anger

- Walking away from a fight

- Dealing with accusations

- Dealing with being left out

- Dealing with peer pressure

- Dealing with fear

- Dealing with the anger of others

This *Stop and Think program* uses a five-step approach for teaching, reinforcing, or using any of the skills mentioned above. The five steps are the following:

1. *Stop and think!* This step is designed to condition children to take the time necessary to calm down and think about how they want to handle a situation.

2. *Are you going to make a good choice or a bad choice?* This step provides children with a chance to decide what kind of choice they want to make. With help from parents, along with the meaningful positive

and negative consequences for various choices, children decide to make a good choice.

3. *What are your choices or steps?* This step helps children develop a specific plan before implementing a social skill. Parents assist children by providing possible good choices or by teaching specific skills by breaking them into their component behavioral parts. This step helps children to think before they act, which gets them ready to move into action.

4. *Just do it!* Here is where children perform their "good choice" behavior. If the specific skill or choice works, that's great. If not, the child is either provided with additional choices by their parents or they are taught a new skill to use. Sometimes, they are prompted to go over the steps of a previously taught skill to make sure that they are using it properly. Once successful, it's on to the last step.

5. *The good job!* This step prompts children to reinforce themselves for successfully using a social skill and successfully responding to a situation or request. This step is important because children—and adults—do not always reinforce themselves for making good choices and doing a good job. Thus, this step teaches self-reinforcement.

This program is part of a larger effort called Project Achieve, which includes teaching parents how to teach children the skills mentioned above. Here's where you can reach that project: http://www.projectachieve.info/stop-think/stop-and-think.html.

Parents on Board

The *Parents on Board* program by Drs. Michael H. Popkin, Bettie B. Youngs, and Jane M. Healy is a parent-involvement-in-education program. It is for parents of four- to fourteen-year-old children, and it assumes that parents want their children to succeed in school but aren't sure how they can help.

The program reinforces parents' motivation for their children's academic success by sharing some important facts from the research on children's academic achievement. The research is very clear that children whose parents are involved in their education

- get better grades,

- do more homework,

- have better attendance,

- have a higher graduation rate, and

- demonstrate a more positive attitude.

The program then goes on to teach parents a set of skills and attitudes on how best to be involved in their children's education. The three teaching sessions cover the following:

Session One: Preparing Your Child to Succeed

- Learning styles

- Learning habits

- Social skills

- Healthy bodies, healthy minds

- Structuring the school-smart home

- Start the year off right

- Maintain a good relationship all year

- Understanding information from the school

- If you suspect a learning difference

Session Two: Encouraging Positive Behavior

- Encouragement

- Discipline

- Beliefs build success

- How to teach a positive belief

Session Three: Reinforcing Your Child's Academic Skills

- Parent as coach

- Coaching your child in reading

- Coaching your child in writing, spelling, math, and science

Parents on Board can be found at http://www. activeparenting.com/POB_main.

There are many other skill-building programs that now exist, each of which teaches a series of excellent skills and strategies. There are more such programs for the parents of young children and for the parents of teenagers. There are programs that focus on specific parenting issues and challenges and similar programs for parents of children with special needs.

The following are brief descriptions of some of these other fine programs.

Active Parenting Programs

These programs were written also by Dr. Michael Popkin. There are several versions of this program, which was the first in the nation to make use of filmed vignettes of effective and ineffective ways of raising children. These include versions for parents of different-aged children (*1, 2, 3, 4 Parents!* for parents of children four and under; *Active Parenting Now* for parents of elementary school age children; and *Active Parenting of Teens*). There are also program versions for parents from Jewish and Christian backgrounds and for parents who are raising children in stepfamilies. In addition, there are programs of different lengths, including single-topic programs that can be taught through lunch-and-learn presentations at work sites and three- and seven-session versions.

These programs exemplify and use the *encouragement method*. Other parenting topics and skills that are taught include the use of *I-Messages* and family meetings. The programs, including an online version, can be accessed at Active Parenting Publishers: www.activeparenting.com

Children in the Middle

This is a program for parents who are going through a divorce or separation. Communication skills are taught to help them learn how to avoid involving their children in loyalty conflicts, which are the most damaging aspect of divorce and separation for children. It is possible to take this and related courses online at the Center for Divorce Education at www.divorce-education.com

Families and Schools Together (FAST)

FAST is a program that brings parents, children, and schools together for a variety of activities, bonding, and togetherness. Ten to twelve families meet for eight weekly sessions for a family meal and a variety of social activities, including music, drawing, family games, children's games, a parent group, and a chance for parents to interact with each other. These activities are fun for the children and families. Participating families engage in communication activities that improve their functioning as family units. The program can be accessed at www.wcer.wisc.edu/fast

Guiding Good Choices

This is a substance-abuse prevention program that was previously known as Preparing for the Drug-Free Years. It teaches parents the skills and information needed to reduce their children's risk for using alcohol and other drugs. Designed for parents of children in grades four to eight (ages nine to fourteen), the program can be found at http://www.sdrg.org/ggc.asp

Parenting Wisely

Parenting Wisely is an interactive CD-ROM program designed for parents of adolescents and preadolescents (ages eight to eighteen). Nine typical problem situations are presented, including doing homework and other chores, improving stepparent-youth relationships, monitoring troublesome friends, improving poor school performance, sibling fighting, and complying with parental requests over phone use and music volume. Both effective and ineffective solutions are depicted for each problem, followed by comprehensive critiques and explanations of the parenting and communication skills viewed. An online version is also available at the program's website: www. familyworksinc.com

Strengthening Families

This fourteen-session parenting and family skill-building program teaches parenting skills, children's life skills, and family life skills. Parents and children participate separately and together. There are special versions for parents with children of different ages, as well as versions for various cultural groups. There is also a home-use DVD version. All can be found at www.strengtheningfamiliesprogram.org

Systematic Training for Effective Parenting (STEP)

These programs teach the *encouragement method* as well as teaching a variety of other skills and strategies, such as the goals of child misbehavior, logical and natural consequences, and family meetings. There are different versions for parents with young children (*Early Childhood STEP*) and parents of teenagers (*STEP Teen*) and the basic *STEP* program for parents of elementary-school children. There are also versions for use in religious settings, as well as a version in Spanish. They can be obtained at www. STEPPUBLISHERS.org

The Incredible Years

This parenting skill-building program is devoted to the challenges of raising children in the four- to eight-year-old age range and especially children who are experiencing behavior problems. It focuses on strengthening parenting competencies (monitoring, positive discipline, confidence) and fostering parents' involvement in children's school experiences to promote their academic and social competencies and reduce conduct problems. There are special versions for parents, children, and teachers. All are available at www.incredibleyears.com

Finding Programs and Helping Professionals

To find an organization in your area that may be offering these programs, call the central telephone number for community referrals, 211. Tell them you are looking for a parenting class in your area. If they find one or more such classes, ask if those classes are in the parenting program you are interested in.

Also, you can contact the program developers themselves to see if they have a list of instructors in your area.

A third option is—if you can't find any of these programs being offered by your local organizations—to give the leaders of those organizations information about the programs and orient them to bring the program to their organization. They can do that by contacting the program developers themselves and asking where they can get a staff member trained to deliver it. Or they can purchase the instructor kit and have one of their staff deliver the program.

Television

The proliferation of cable and pay-per-view channels has made television an extremely helpful vehicle for learning about effective parenting and child development. Television always had some programming directed toward parents, and now there are more channels through which you can gain such education.

In addition, news broadcasts often have segments on tips for parents where the stations contact parenting experts to provide guidance and convey information on parenting through sound bites. The value of such programming is evidenced by the fact that these parenting news features often air during the times when the television stations have the most to gain from having as large a viewership as possible—the "sweep" periods when a larger audience can influence how much stations can charge for advertising time.

Specific programs that are devoted to effective parenting are excellent ways to learn—the various *Supernanny* shows are good examples. The wise nannies who are dispatched to do their special type of home-visiting parenting education employ methods and principles that are taught in many of the parenting skill-building programs that we have learned about. They are extremely creative practitioners who convey sophisticated ideas in ways that are easy to comprehend.

Another popular show that provides very personalized and dramatic examples of both ineffective and effective parenting is the *Dr. Phil* show. Dr. Phil draws on his personal and professional experiences as a practicing psychologist to help parents and families that are in distress and hurting each other. He provides perspective on what these families are doing to perpetuate their problems and then offers guidance on how these problems can be better addressed. The guidance includes learning and using better parenting and human relations skills—the same types of skills that are taught in modern parenting and family programs.

Parenting Magazines

In addition to the venerable *Parents Magazine,* there are other fine magazines that provide excellent articles and tips on parenting. There are also parenting magazines for specific populations of parents, such as *Working Mothers* magazine.

Other print media resources that are now available include parenting newspapers that you can obtain at newsstands and newspaper boxes in the front of markets and children's stores. These publications usually reflect their local nature, such as *LA Parent*, *Seattle Child*, or *New York Family*. Each of these publications provides a unique resource for parents, educators, professionals, and childcare providers. They supply information on what to do and where to go with children in their own town, school district, and neighborhood.

Regular features include a monthly calendar of events for children and their parents, practical advice for parents, information about outings, and reviews of current plays, movies, books, and local restaurants. Feature articles discuss a range of important issues that affect families, from prenatal care to teenage parties.

These regional publications have their own organization, the *Parenting Publications of America*. You can search for the parenting newspaper in your area by going to the organization's website (www.parentingpublications.org) and entering your state in the search section.

Using the Internet

We twenty-first-century parents are fortunate because of the existence of the Internet. As you have been informed, all the top parenting and family skill-building programs have websites where you can learn about them and become connected. In addition, as you have learned, a few of those fine programs can be taken over the Internet.

The resources mentioned here barely scratch the surface of what is available on the Internet to assist you with raising your children.

By going to a search engine such as Google.com, you will find at least 273 million websites about parenting! Many of these websites are outstanding. They help answer just about any question you might have about parenting, and they include chat rooms and bulletin boards where you can correspond electronically with other parents and parenting experts. Websites of a comprehensive nature, such as www.babycenter.com and www.parentcenter.com, also allow you to receive a regular parenting newsletter that is geared to the specific age of your child.

However, many parenting websites are of minimal or little value. The challenge is to find those that are going to be most beneficial to you in your unique parenting situation. Fortunately, some thoughtful and responsible organizations have taken the time and energy to evaluate the enormous number of parenting websites and recommend the ones they consider to be exemplary. The best of these guides is probably Tufts University Child and Family Web Guide, www.cfw.tufts.edu.

This web guide is a directory that evaluates, describes, and provides links to hundreds of sites containing child development research and practical advice. It was created and is operated by the Eliot-Pearson Department of Child Development at Tufts University. It was initiated because many parenting websites provide information that is not consistent with child development research. This resource guides viewers toward those sites that provide research-based parenting advice. It is based on parent and professional feedback, as well as support from noted child development experts such as David Elkind, Edward Zigler, and the late Fred Rogers. It includes major sections on family/parenting, education/learning, typical child development, health/mental health, and resources/ recreation.

I also strongly recommend the website of CICC to which you have already been oriented. It now has a blog page that publishes very helpful articles on parenting, such as "Why We Must Stop Hitting Children" and "Safety Rules" to share with children about what they should do if they are stopped by the police. You can easily assure yourself that you will automatically receive these articles by signing up for CICC's mailing list. You can do this on the home page for the website (www.ciccparenting.org) by scrolling to the middle of the page where you will find a sign-up form.

Finding a Psychotherapist

Here too the Internet can be of great assistance.

If you have decided that your multiyear parenting errors are based on your just not being a very positive person in general, visits for psychotherapy are very much in order. And making such visits also requires a good deal of personal courage.

I suggest you start by talking to people you know and trust. Talking to a friend or a family member about their therapist might help you better understand whether that person would be helpful to you. Your family physician might also know professionals they respect and trust. Since a lot of people's healthcare choices will be decided based upon whether that professional is a part of their healthcare plan or not, check with your insurance or healthcare provider to get a list of approved professionals.

Online databases are also a valuable resource to research, as they will often provide a little more information than your local yellow pages. There are online databases for *psychologists, marriage child and family therapists*, and *psychiatrists*. Some of these databases allow the professional to enhance their listing with additional information, such as experience, educational degrees, and ways they prefer to work. This can be helpful in finding professionals who have specific backgrounds or experience with specific kinds of issues like your parenting-related issues.

Keep in mind that throughout this process, it's best to keep an open mind and not to necessarily go with the first professional you see. Choosing a professional that's going to be helpful to you and your needs is often much like a job-interview process—you need to find one that's going to work with you and for you and that you feel most comfortable with.

There are also many different types of psychotherapy. Here are some that you can learn about by entering their name in any search engine:

- Behavior therapy
- Cognitive therapy

- Dialectical behavior therapy

- Psychodynamic therapy

- Gestalt therapy

- Group therapy

- Family therapy

- Mindfulness-based therapy

Again, by seeking out and obtaining the most relevant type of psychotherapy for yourself, you will be taking more positive actions to become the best person you can be in relating to your children.

Conclusion

So now my fellow parents, you have learned about the type of errors we all make in raising our children. They are very common as they are part of the territory of being a parent.

You have been exposed to the *AAR approach* to solving these errors. And hopefully you have chosen to apply this approach.

You have also been exposed to numerous ways of developing and maintaining positive and sensitive relations to your children (and with other people as well).

I sincerely hope you take advantage of all this to do the best parenting job possible. When we as parents are doing the best, we are helping ourselves and our children to lead better lives.

In addition, we are also helping our entire nation, because effectively and sensitively raised children are the most likely to grow up to be productive adults and effective parents themselves.

Indeed, when we parents are maximally effective in raising children, our nation benefits in numerous ways. Effective parenting helps diminish social and health problems and promote all sorts of wonderful societal accomplishments.

Benefits of Effective Parenting

May you experience the best results for you, your children, your family, and for our society!

I look forward to hearing from you about your experiences with the *AAR approach*, and I extend my sincerest respect and appreciation for your taking the time to read this book.

Index

Audience

The book is written for *all* parents, whether biological, foster, adoptive, step or grandparents—including parents of adult children.

Genre

The book is written as a general public book, rather than as a book for professionals in the parenting and related fields. It is the type of book that such professionals are likely to want to make available to their clients who are parents and to their own family members, friends and professional colleagues.

Acknowledgements

This book is based on my nearly 50 years of experiences as a psychotherapist and parent educator. It is also based on my wonderful experiences in helping to raise our daughters, Lisa and Britt. Those experiences were part of a marriage of 30 years to their mother, and my ex-wife, Mary.

The actual writing of this book was facilitated by my very talented cousin, Sharon Benson, who now works for our organization, the Center for the Improvement of Child Caring. Sharon has been lovingly supportive and helpfully critical throughout. Her enthusiasm, energy and talent has been invaluable in completing this book.